C

easy learning
Arabic
phrasebook

Consultant
S.Abdi-Goulid

First published 2007
This edition published 2010
Copyright © HarperCollins Publishers
Reprint 10 9 8 7 6 5 4 3 2 1 0
Typeset by Davidson Pre-Press, Glasgow
Printed in Malaysia for Imago

www.collinslanguage.com

ISBN 978-0-00-735849-6

Using your phrasebook

Your *Collins Gem Phrasebook* is designed to help you locate the exact phrase you need, when you need it, whether on holiday or for business. If you want to adapt the phrases, you can easily see where to substitute your own words using the dictionary section, and the clear, full-colour layout gives you direct access to the different topics.

The Gem Phrasebook includes:
- Over 70 topics arranged thematically. Each phrase is accompanied by a simple pronunciation guide which eliminates any problems pronouncing foreign words.

- A top ten tips section to safeguard against any cultural faux pas, giving essential dos and don'ts for situations involving local customs or etiquette.

- Practical hints to make your stay trouble free, showing you where to go and what to do when dealing with everyday matters such as travel or hotels and offering valuable tourist information.

- Face to face sections so that you understand what is being said to you. These example mini-dialogues give you a good idea of what to expect from a real conversation.

- Common announcements and messages you may hear, ensuring that you never miss the important information you need to know when out and about.

- A clearly laid-out dictionary means you will never be stuck for words.

- A basic grammar section which will enable you to build on your phrases.

- A list of public holidays to avoid being caught out by unexpected opening and closing hours, and to make sure you don't miss the celebrations!

It's worth spending time before you embark on your travels just looking through the topics to see what is covered and becoming familiar with what might be said to you.

Whatever the situation, your *Gem Phrasebook* is sure to help!

Contents

Pronouncing Arabic

The Arabic alphabet is written and read from right to left and horizontally. There are 28 letters in the Arabic alphabet:

Name of letter	Arabic Letter	Name of letter	Arabic Letter
Taa (t)	ط	alif (ǎ)	أ
Thaa (th)	ظ	Baa (b)	ب
'ein (')	ع	Taa (t)	ت
Qain (q)	غ	Thaa (th)	ث
Faa (f)	ك	Jeem (j)	ج
Qaaf (q)	ق	Haa (h)	ح
Kaaf (k)	ك	Khaa (kh)	خ
Laam (l)	ل	Daal (da)	د
Miim (m)	م	Thaal (th)	ذ
Nuun (n)	ن	Raa (r)	ر
Haa (h)	ه	Zaa (z)	ز
Waaw (w)	و	Seen (s)	س
Yaa (y)	ي	Sheen (sh)	ش
		Saad (s)	ص
		dhaad (dh)	ض

The table below shows the letters that are similar to those in English, and that you should therefore have no problem learning or pronouncing.

Name of letter	Arabic letter	Sounds like	Name of letter	Arabic letter	Sounds like
Alif (ă)	ا	apple	Saad (s)	ص	sorry
Baa (b)	ب	ball	Taa (t)	ط	tip
Taa (t)	ت	ticket	Thaa (th)	ظ	thaw
Thaa (th)	ث	thick	Faa (f)	ف	far
Jeem (j)	ج	jam	Kaaf (k)	ك	cat
Daal (da)	د	done	Laam (l)	ل	lot
Thaal (th)	ذ	though	Miim (m)	م	mother
Raa (r)	ر	rat	Nuun (n)	ن	nun
Zaa (z)	ز	zoo	Haa (h)	ه	hand
Seen (s)	س	sad	Waaw (w)	و	wood
Sheen (sh)	ش	shop	Yaa (y)	ي	yes

Unfamiliar sounds

....

The Arabic letters below are the ones that are either hard to pronounce or are pronounced a little bit differently.

Name of letter	Arabic letter	Sounds like
Haa (h)	ح	Similar to **h** in house
Khaa (kh)	خ	Similar to **ch** in loch
'ein (')	ع	Similar to **a** in another
Ghain (q)	غ	Similar to a French **r** sound
Qaaf (q)	ق	Like **q** but a little bit sharper

Top ten tips

• •

There are some social conventions and local customs that visitors should be aware of when travelling in Arab countries. Many traditional customs and beliefs are tied up with religion, and Islam (the main religion in most Arab countries) has a clear influence on how people live and behave.

1   A handshake is the customary form of greeting.

2   Many of the manners and social customs are similar to French manners, particularly amongst the middle classes.

3   Visitors may find, in some social situations, that being patient and firm pays dividends.

4   Often, visitors may find themselves the centre of unsolicited attention. In towns, young boys after money will be eager to point out directions, sell goods or simply charge for a photograph, while unofficial guides will offer advice or services. Visitors should be courteous, but wary of the latter.

5 Women travelling alone, and/or wearing clothes regarded as procavative (e.g. revealing tops, short skirts, etc.) may attract unwanted attention.

6 Sexual relations outside marriage, and homosexual conduct are punishable by law.

7 Smoking is widespread and it is customary to offer cigarettes. In most cases it is obvious where not to smoke, except during Ramadan when it is illegal to eat, drink or smoke in public.

8 Dress should be conservative and women should not wear revealing clothes, particularly when in religious buildings and in towns. Western style clothing is, however, accepted in modern nightclubs, restaurants, hotels and bars in tourist destinations.

9 In Egypt tourists have to pay a fee to take photographs inside pyramids, tombs and museums.

10 Alcohol is tolerated, with non-Muslims allowed to drink alcohol in the city bars, restaurants, clubs and hotels.

Talking to people

Hello/goodbye, yes/no

Body language is very important when dealing with Arabs. You will see that when they talk, they often use their hands to describe what they are saying.

Please	من فضلك min fadlak
Thank you	شكرا لك shuk-ran laka
Thanks	شكرا shuk-ran
Yes	نعم na-'am

13

| No | لا |
| | la |

Sorry! | آسف!
aa-sif

Excuse me! | لو سمحت!
law sa-mah-t!

Hello/Hi | مرحبا/سلام
mar-ha-ba/salaam

Goodbye | الى اللقاء/مع السلامة
ilal-li-qaa/ma-'as-sa-laa-ma

Good morning | صباح الخير
sa-baa-hul-khayr

Good afternoon | مساء الخير
ma-sa-ul-khayr

Good day | نهار سعيد
na-haar sa-'iid

Good evening | مساء الخير
ma-sa-ul-khayr

14

| Goodnight | ليلة سعيدة |
| | lay-la-tun sa-'ii-da |

| I don't | لم أفهم |
| understand | lam af-ham |

| I don't speak | لا اتكلم العربية |
| Arabic | laa af-ha-mul-'a-ra-biy-ya |

Key phrases

. . . .

| Is there...?/ | هل هناك...؟ |
| Are there...? | hal hu-naa-ka...? |

| Do you have...? | هل عندك...؟ |
| | hal 'in-da-ka...? |

| Do you have | هل عندك خبز؟ |
| bread? | hal 'in-da-ka khubz? |

| Do you have | هل عندك حليب؟ |
| milk? | hal 'in-da-ka halib? |

15

| Do you have stamps? | هل عندك طوابع بريد؟ |
| | hal 'in-da-ka ta-waa-bi' ba-rii-diy-ya? |

| I want/need... | أنا أريد.... |
| | anaa u-rii-du... |

| I want a loaf | أنا أريد رغيفا |
| | anaa u-rii-du ra-ghifan |

| I want this | أنا أريد هذا |
| | anaa u-rii-du haa-thaa |

| I don't want this | لا أريد هذا |
| | laa u-rii-du haa-thaa |

| How much is this? | بكم هذا؟ |
| | bi-kem haa-thaa? |

| How many? | كم واحدة؟ |
| | kem waa-hi-da? |

| When is...? | متى....؟ |
| | ma-taa...? |

When is breakfast?	متى وقت الفطور؟ ma-taa waq-tul fu-tuur?
What time is it?	كم الساعة؟ kem as-saa-'ah?
At what time...?	في أي ساعة...؟ fii ay-yi saa-'ah...?
Where is...?	أين...؟ ay-na...?
Where is the bank?	أين البنك؟ ay-nal bank?
Where is the toilet?	أين المرحاض؟ ay-nal mir-haad?
Which one?	أي واحد؟ ay-yu waa-hid?
Why?	لماذا؟ li-maa-thaa?
Please go away!	أتركني لو سمح! ut-ruk-nii law sa-mah-t!

Is...included?	هل ... في الحساب؟ hal ... fil hi-saab?
a/an/one ... please	واحدة من فضلك ... ... waa-hida min fad-lak
two teas please	كأسين شاي من فضلك ka' sein shai min fad-lak
some ... please	قليل من ... من فضلك qa-liil min ... min fad-lak

Signs and notices

مفتوح	maf-tuuh	open
مغلق	muqlaq	closed
سيدات	say-yidaat	ladies
رجال	ri-jaal	gentlemen
خدمة ذاتية	khidma thaa-tiy-yah	self-service
ادفع	id-fa'	push
اسحب	is-hab	pull
المحاسب	al-mu-haasib	cash desk

ماء شرب	maa shurb	drinking water
مراحيض	maraa-hiid	toilets
شاغر	shaaqir	vacant
مشغول	mash-quul	engaged
جناح الطوارئ	janaahut-tawaari	emergency department
الإسعافات الأولية	al-is'aafaa-tul-aw-waliy-ya	first aid
ممتلئ	mumta-li	full
قف	qif	stop
معطل	mu'attal	out of order
للإيجار	lil-iijaar	for hire/rent
للبيع	lil-bay-'	for sale
تنزيلات	tan-ziilaat	sales
الطابق تحت الأرض	at-taabiq tahtal-ard	basement
الطابق الأرضي	at-taabiq al-ardii	ground floor
دخول	du-khuul	entrance
مكتب التذاكر	maktabut-tathaakir	ticket office
محطة الشرطة	mahata-tush-shur-tah	police station

الأشياء الضائعة	al-ash-yaa ad-daa-i-'ah	lost property
مغادرة/ إقلاع	muqadarah/ iqlaa'	departures
وصول	wusuul	arrivals
ممنوع	mamnuu'	prohibited
الحقائب المتركة	al-haqaa-ib al-matruukah	left luggage
خاص	khaas	private
ساخن	saakhin	hot
بارد	baarid	cold
خطر	khatar	danger
ممنوع التدخين	mam-nuu-'ut-tadkhiin	no smoking
لا تلمس	laa talmas	do not touch
خروج	khuruuj	exit
غرفة تغيير الملابس	qurfat taq-yiir al-malaabis	changing room
الحمام	al-ham-maam	bathroom
احذر!	ih-thar!	caution!
معلومات	ma'-luumaat	information
استعلامات	isti'-laamaat	enquiries

Polite expressions

As in every culture, good manners are very important to Arabs. You may experience excessive politeness when people meet each other. Hugging and kissing on both cheeks is very normal. People often kiss the hand of elderly people out of respect. To address someone formally, use **as-say-yid** for men or **as-say-yida** for women before their first name, for example, **As-say-yid Ahmed**; **As-say-yida Faatima**. This may vary from country to country.

There are several styles of greeting in use; it is best to wait for your counterpart to initiate the greeting. Men shake hands with other men. Some men will shake hands with women, however, it is advisable for businesswomen to wait for a man to offer his hand. A more traditional greeting between men involves grasping each other's right hand, placing the left hand on the other's right shoulder and exchanging kisses on each cheek.

How do you do? كيف حالك؟
kay-fa haa-luk?

Pleased to meet you	أنا سعيد لرؤيتك
	anaa sa-'ii-dun li ru-ya-ti-ka
Thank you	شكرا لك
	shuk-ran laka
I am fine	أنا بخير
	ana bi-khayr
Welcome!	أهلا و سهلا!
	ah-lan wa sah-lan!
Here you are	تفضل
	tafad-dal
Pardon?	عذراً
	'uth-ran
This is...	هذا... / هذه...
	haa-thaa ... (m)/haa-thihii (f)
This is my husband	هذا زوجي
	haa-thaa zaw-jii
This is my wife	هذه زوجتي
	haa-thi-hii zaw-jatii

Enjoy your meal!	وجبة هنية! waj-ba ha-niy-yah!
The meal was delicious	كانت وجبتاً لذيذة kaa-nat waj-batan la-thii-thah
Thank you very much	شكراً جزيلاً لك shuk-ran ja-ziilan lak
Have a good trip!	رحلة سعيدة! rih-la sa-'iidah!
Enjoy your holiday!	عطلة ممتعة! 'ut-la-tun mum-ti'ah!

Celebrations

. . . .

Happy birthday!	عيد ميلاد سعيد! 'ied-mii-laad sa-'iid!
Congratulations!	مبروك! mab-ruuk!

| Cheers! | هنيئا |
| | han-nii-an |

| Happy New Year! | عام جديد سعيد! |
| | 'aa-mun ja-dii-dun sa-'iid! |

Making friends

| What's your name? | ماسمك؟ |
| | mas-muk? |

| My name is... | اسمي ... |
| | is-mii... |

| How old are you? | كم عمرك؟ |
| | kem 'um-ruka? |

| I'm ... years old | أنا ... سنة |
| | anaa ... sa-nah |

| Where do you live? | أين تسكن؟ |
| | ay-na tas-kun? |

I live...	أنا أسكن ...
	anaa as-ku-nu...

in London	في لندن
	fii len-den

in Australia	في أستراليا
	fii australia

Where are you from?	من أين أنت؟
	min ay-na anta?

I'm English	أنا إنجليزي
	ana inglezi

I'm Canadian	أنا كندي
	ana kanadi

Are you married?	هل أنت متزوج؟
	hal anta mu-ta-zaw-wij?

Do you have children?	هل لديك أطفال؟
	hal la-day-ka at-faal?

I have children	عندي أطفال
	'in-dii at-faal

I don't have children

ليس عندي أطفال

lay-sa 'in-dii at-faal

I have a boyfriend

عندي صديق

'in-dii sa-diiq

I have a girlfriend

عندي صديقة

'in-dii sa-dii-qah

I'm single

أنا عازب

anaa 'a-zib

I'm married

أنا متزوج

anaa mu-ta-zaw-wij

I'm divorced

أنا مطلق/مطلقة

anaa mu-tal-liq (m) mu-tal-laqa (f)

Work

. . . .

What is your job?

ما وظيفتك؟

maa wa-thii-fa-tuk?

> **Leisure/beach** (p 84) > **Sport** (p 90)

| Do you enjoy it? | هل تستمتع بها؟ |
| | hal tas tam ti'u bi-ha? |

| I'm a doctor | أنا (طبيب) دكتور |
| | anaa ta-biib (dok-toor) |

| I'm a teacher | أنا معلم |
| | anaa mu-'al-lim |

| I'm a nurse | أنا ممرض |
| | anaa mu-mar-rid |

| I work in a shop | أنا أعمل في دكان |
| | anaa a'-ma-lu fii duk-kaan |

| I work in a factory | أنا أعمل في مصنع |
| | anaa a'-ma-lu fii mas-na' |

| I work in a bank | أنا أعمل في بنك |
| | anaa a'-ma-lu fii bank |

| I work from home | أنا أعمل من البيت |
| | anaa a'-ma-lu minal-bayt |

Work

Weather

مشرق	mush-riq	clear
ممطر	mum-tir	rainy
بارد	baa-rid	cold
حار	haa-r	hot
مُشمس	mush-mis	sunny

It's sunny

يوم مشمس
yaw-mun mush-mis

It's raining

يوم ممطر
yaw-mun mum-tir

It's windy

يوم عاصف
yaw-mun 'aa-sif

It's very hot

يوم حار جداً
yaw-mun haar jid-dan

What is the temperature?

ما هي درجة الحرارة؟
maa hiya dara-ja-tul ha-raa-rah?

What is the
weather forecast
for tomorrow?

ما هي النشرة الجوية غداً؟

maa hiya an-nash-ra-tul-jaw-wiy-
ya-tu qa-dan?

Does it get cool
at night?

هل تصبح باردة في الليل؟

hal tus-bi-hu baa-ri-dah fil-lay-l!

Will there be a
storm?

هل ستكون هناك عاصفة؟

hal sa-ta-kuu-nu hu-naa-ka
'aa-sifa?

What beautiful
weather!

ما أجمل الطقس!

maa aj-ma-lat-taq-s!

What awful
weather!

ما اسوء الطقس!

maa as-wa-at-taqs!

Getting around

Asking the way

يسار ya-saa-r	left
يمين ya-miin	right
على طول 'alaa tuul	straight on
قريب من qa-riib min	next to
مقابل mu-qaa-bil	opposite
إشارة مرور ishaa-ra-tu mu-ruur	traffic lights
عند المنعطف 'in-dal mun-'ataf	at the corner

FACE TO FACE

لو سمحت، أين مكتب البريد؟
law sa-mah-ta, ay-na mak-ta-bul-ba-riid
Excuse me! Where is the post office?

استمر إلى الأمام ثم انعطف إلى اليمين عند المنعطف
is-tamir ilal-amaam thum-ma in-atif ilal-yamiin 'in-dal mun-'ataf
Keep straight on and turn right at the corner

هل هو بعيد؟
hal hu-wa ba-'iid
Is it far?

٢ دقائق فقط
da-qii-qa-taan fa-qat
Two minutes away

شكراً لك
shuk-ran laka
Thank you

على الرحب و السعة
'a-lar-rahb was-sa'ah
You are welcome

Where is...?	أين...
	ay-na...
Where is the museum?	أين المتحف؟
	ay-nal mit-haf?

31

How do I get...?	كيف أصل إلى.....؟
	key-fa asi-lu ilaa...?
How do I get to the museum?	كيف أصل إلى المتحف؟
	key-fa asi-lu ila-l mit-haf?
to the coach station	إلى محطة الباص
	ilaa ma-hat-tat al-baas
to the beach	إلى الشاطئ
	ila-sh-shaa-ti
to my hotel	إلى فندقي
	ilaa fun-du-qii
Is it far?	هل هو بعيد؟
	hal hu-wa ba-'iid?

YOU MAY HEAR...	
انحن/لِف يسار in-hani/lif ya-saar	Turn left
انحن/لِف يمين in-hani/lif ya-miin	Turn right
استمر إلى الأمام is-ta-mir ila-l amaam	Keep straight on

Bus and coach

In some Arab countries, if you are male, you will have to take a seat at the rear of the bus and leave the front seats for the female passengers.

باص أو حافلة	baas/hafila	coach/bus
موقف الباص	maw-qif al-baas	bus stop
محطة الباصات ma-hat-tat al-baa-saat		coach station
تذكرة	that-karah	ticket

FACE TO FACE

A لو سمحت. أين الباص المقلع في الساعة السابعة صباحاً إلى القاهرة؟

law sa-mah-t. Ay-nal-baas al-muq-li'
fis-saa'atis-saabi-'ah sa-baa-han ilaa Al-qaa-hi-ra?

Excuse me. Which one is the 7 o'clock bus to Cairo?

B الباص على اليمين. الباص الأزرق

al-baas 'a-laal-ya-miin. al-baas al-az-raq

The one on the right. The blue bus.

A شكرا

shukran

Thanks

33

| Where is the coach station? | أين محطة الباصات؟ |
| | ay-na ma-hat-tat al-baa-saat? |

| I am going to... | أنا ذاهب إلى... |
| | anaa thaa-hi-bun ilaa... |

| Is there a bus to...? | هل هناك باص إلى... |
| | hal hu-naa-ka baas-sun ilaa... |

| Does it go to...? | هل يذهب إلى... |
| | hal yath-ha-bu ilaa... |

| to the airport | إلى المطار |
| | ilal-mataar |

| to the beach | إلى الشاطئ |
| | ilash-shaati |

| to the centre | إلى مركز المدينة |
| | ilaa mar-kaz al-ma-dii-nah |

| one ticket | تذكرة واحدة |
| | tath-ka-ra-tun waa-hida |

| two tickets | تذكرتان |
| | tath-ka-ra-taan |

34

| three tickets | ٣ تذاكر
tha-laa-thu ta-thaa-kir | |

| When is the next bus? | متى يصل الباص التالي؟
ma-taa ya-si-lul baa-sut-taa-lii? | |

YOU MAY HEAR...

| لا يوجد باص
laa yuu-ja-du baas | There is no bus |
| يجب أن تأخذ سيارة أجرة
ya-ji-b an ta-khu-tha
say-yaa-ra-ta uj-ra | You must take a taxi |

Metro

Cairo has got a metro system.

| مدخل mad-khal | entrance |
| مخرج makh-raj | way out |

> **Luggage** (p 111)

Where is the nearest metro station?	أين أقرب محطة مترو (أنفاق)؟ ay-na aq-rab ma-hat-tat metro (an-faaq)?
How does the ticket machine work?	كيف تُستخدَم آلة التذاكر؟ kay-fa tus-takh-dam aa-lat at-ta-thaa-kir?
Do you have a map of the metro?	هل لديك خريطة للمترو؟ hal la-day-ka kha-rii-ta lil metro?
I'm going to...	أنا ذاهب إلى... anaa thaa-hib ilaa...
How do I/we get to...?	كيف أصل إلى... kay-fa a-si-lu ilaa...
Do I have to change?	هل يجب علي أن أغير الحافلة؟ hal ya-ji-bu 'a-lay-ya an u-qay-yira al-haafila?
What is the next stop?	ما هو الموقف التالي؟ maa hu-wa al-maw qif at-taa-lii?

36

Excuse me! I'm getting off here	لو سمحت! أنا نازل هنا
	law sa-mah-t! anaa naa-zil hunaa

Please let me through	لو سمحت، دعني أمر
	law sa-mah-t, da'-nii amur

Train

محطة	ma-hat-ta	station
قطار	qi-taar	train
منصة	mi-nas-sa	platform
مقعد	maq-'ad	seat
تذكرة	that-ka-ra	ticket
مكتب الحجز mak-tab al-haj-z		booking office
جدول مواعيد jad-wal ma-waa-'iid		timetable
وصلة	was-lah	connection

Getting around

A متى موعد القطار التالي إلى إزمر؟

ma-taa maw-'id al-qi-taar at-taa-lii ilaa Monastir?

When is the next train to Monastir?

B في الساعة السابعة

fis-saa-'a-tis saa-bi-'a

At 7 o'clock

A ثلاثة تذاكر من فضلك

tha-laa-tha-tu ta-thaa-kir min fad-lak

Three tickets please

B ذهاب (فقط) أم ذهاب و إياب؟

tha-haab (fa-qat) am tha-haab wa i-yaab?

Single or return?

A ذهاب و إياب، من فضلك

tha-haab wa i-yaab min fad-lak

Return please

Where is the station?	أين المحطة؟ ay-nal ma-hat-ta?
a single	تذكرة واحدة ذهاب فقط tath-ka-ra waa-hi-da tha-haab fa-qat

two singles	تذكرتان ذهاب فقط that-ka-ra-taan tha-haab fa-qat
a single to Monastir	تذكرة ذهاب فقط إلى ازمير that-ka-rat tha-haab fa-qat ilaa Monastir
two singles to Alexandria	تذكرتان ذهاب فقط إلى الاسكندرية that-ka-ra-taan tha-haab fa-qat ilaa Alexandria
a return	تذكرة واحدة ذهاب و إياب that-ka-ra waa-hida tha-haab wa i-yaab
two returns	تذكرتان ذهاب و إياب that-ka-ra-taan tha-haab wa i-yaab
one adult	بالغ واحد baa-liq waa-hid
two children	طفلان tif-laan

two adults	بالغان
	baa-li-qaan

first class	درجة اولى
	da-ra-jah uu-laa

second class	درجة ثانية
	da-ra-jah thaa-ni-yah

smoking	المدخنين
	qayr al-mu-da-khi-niin

non-smoking	غير المدخنين
	al-mu-da-khi-niin

I want to book a seat	أريد أن أحجز مقعدا
	u-rii-du an ah-jiza maq-'adan

Which platform?	أيُّ رصيف؟
	ay-yu ra-siif?

When does it get to Cairo?	متى سيصل القاهرة؟
	ma-taa sa-ya-si-lu Al Qahira?

When does it leave?	متى يغادر؟
	ma-taa yu-qaa-dir?

| When does it arrive? | متى يصل؟ |
| | ma-taa ya-sil? |

| Is this seat free? | هل هذا المقعد شاغر؟ |
| | hal haa-thal-maq-'ad shaa-qir? |

| Excuse me! | آسف! |
| | aa-sif! |

| Occupied | مأخوذ |
| | ma-khuu-th |

Taxi

There are plenty of taxis in cities, towns and resorts. It is always wise to check the price before a long journey. Taxis can be shared, which is a cheaper option, but you will have to wait until all the seats are occupied. Taxi in Arabic is also 'taxi', but you might also hear 'uj-rah' which literally means 'hire'. 'Taxi' is used throughout the following section. Alternatively, there are minibuses which provide transport over short distances.

> **Luggage** (p 111)

Where can I get a taxi?	أين أجد تاكسي؟
	ay-na a-ji-du taksi?
I want to go to...	أريد الذهاب إلى ...
	u-rii-du ath-tha-haa-ba ilaa...
How much is it?	كم قيمتها؟
	kam qii-ma-tu-haa?
To the airport, please	إلى المطار من فضلك
	ilal-ma-taar min fad-lak
To the beach, please	إلى الشاطئ من فضلك
	ilash-shaa-ti min fad-lak
Please stop here	قف هنا لو سمحت
	qif-hunaa law sa-mah-t
Please wait	انتظر لو سمحت
	in-ta-thir law sa-mah-t
It's too expensive	هذا غالي جداً
	haa-thaa qaa-li jid-dan
I've no change	ليس عندي صرف
	lay-saa 'in-dii sarf
Keep the change	خذ الباقي
	khuth al-baa-qii

Boat and ferry

Boats and ferries are not considered a main mode of transport in most of the Arab world. Occasionally small boats are used to cross canals and rivers in some countries such as Egypt. This is due to the fact that most Arab countries do not have canal or river systems.

مكتب التذاكر mak-tab at-ta-thaa-kir	ticket office
تذكرة للعبّارة that-ka-ra lil-'ab-baa-rah	token for ferry
جدول المواعيد jad-wal al-ma-waa-'iid	timetable
الوصول al-wu-suul	arrival
المغادرة al-mu-qaa-da-ra	departure
القارب المزعنف al-qaa-rib al-mu-za'-naf	hydrofoil

one token	تذكرة واحدة
	tath-ka-ra waa-hi-da
two tokens	تذكرتان
	that-ka-ra-taan
three tokens	ثلاث تذاكر
	tha-laa-thu ta-thaa-kir
When is the next boat?	متى المركب القادم؟
	ma-tal mar-ka-bul qaa-dim?
When is the last boat?	متى المركب الأخير؟
	ma-tal mar-ka-bul a-khii-r?
Is there a hydrofoil?	هَلْ هناك قارب مزعنف؟
	hal hu-naa-ka qaa-rib mu-za'-naf?
We want to go to...	نُريدُ الذهاب إلى ...
	nu-rii-duth-tha-haa-ba ila...
Is there a timetable?	هَلْ هناك جدول مواعيد؟
	hal hu-naa-ka jad-wal ma-waa-'iid?

When does the boat leave?	متى يرحل المركب؟	ma-taa yar-ha-lu al-mar-kab?
How long does it take?	كَمْ مِنَ الوقت يأخذَ؟	kam min al-waq-ti ya-khu-th?

Air travel

المطار	al-ma-taar	airport
البوابة	al-baw-waa-ba	gate
القادمون	al-qaa-di-muun	arrivals
المغادرة	al-mu-qaa-da-rah	departures
الطيران	at-ta-ya-raan	flight
محلي	ma-hal-li	domestic
دولي	du-wa-li	international
المعلومات	al-ma'-luu-maat	information

To the airport, please	إلى المطار، رجاءً	ilal ma-taar, ra-jaa-an
My flight is at ... o'clock	طيارتي في الساعة ...	tay-yaa-ra-tii fis-saa-'a ...

45

How much is it to the airport?	كَمْ التسعيرة إلى المطارِ؟ kam at-tas-'ii-rah ilal ma-taar?
How much is it to the town centre?	كَمْ التسعيرة إلى مركز البلدة؟ kam at-tas-'ii-rah ilaa mar-kaz al ma-dii-na?
When will the flight leave?	متى تقلع الطائرة؟ ma-taa tuq-li-'ut-taa-ira?

YOU MAY HEAR...

إذهبْ إلى البوابة رقم... ith-hab ilal-baw-waa-bah ra-qam...	Go to gate number...

> **Luggage** (p 111)

Customs control

The import, export, possession and use of drugs is strictly forbidden and penalties for offenders are extremely severe.

جواز السفر ja-waa-z as-sa-far	passport
جمارك ja-maa-rik	customs
خمر/كحول khamr/ku-huul	alcohol
دخان dukh-khaan (you may also hear: تبغ = tabq)	tobacco

Do I have to pay duty on this?   هلْ عليَّ أنْ أدْفعَ ضريبةَ على هذه؟
hal 'a-lay-ya an ad-fa'a da-rii-bah 'a-laa haa-thaa?

It is my medicine   إنه دوائي
in-na-huu da-waa-ii

I bought this duty-free   إشتريتُ هذا غير خاضع للضريبة
ish-ta-ray-tu haa-thaa al-qayr khaa-di' lid-da-rii-bah

47

Driving

Car hire

مفاتيح ma-faa-tiih	keys
وثائق التأمين wa-thaa-iq at-ta-miin	insurance documents
رخصة القيادة rukh-satul-qi-yaa-dah	driving licence

I want to hire
a car

أريدُ إستئجار سيارة
u-rii-du is-ti-gaar say-yaarah

with automatic
gears

بالجير (تروس) الآلية
bil-gear (tu-ruus) al-aali

for one day

ليوم واحد
li yawm waa-hid

for two days

ليومين
li yaw-mayn

| How much is it? | كم قيمتها؟ |
| | kam qii-ma-tu-haa? |

| Is insurance included? | هل هذا يتضمن التأمين؟ |
| | hal haa-thaa ya-ta-dam-man at-ta-miin? |

| Is there a deposit to pay? | هل هناك ايداع للدفع؟ |
| | hal hu-naa-ka ii-daa' lid-daf'? |

| Can I pay by credit card? | هل من الممكن أن أدفع بالبطاقة الائتمانية؟ |
| | hal mi-nal mum-kin an ad-fa'a bil-bi-taa-qah al-i-ti-maa-ni-yah? |

| What petrol does it take? | ما نوع الوقود؟ |
| | maa naw-'ul wa-quud? |

Car hire

Driving and petrol

انتبه/خطر in-ta-bih/kha-tar	caution/danger
قف qif	stop
خط سريع khat sa-rii'	motorway
مركز المدينة mar-kaz al-ma-dii-nah	town centre

Can I park here?
هل مسموح أن أقف هنا؟
hal mas-muu-h an a-qi-fa huna?

How long can
I park for?
إلى متى ممكن أقف هنا؟
ila ma-taa mum-kin a-qif hunaa?

We are driving
to...
نحن ذاهبون إلى...
nah-nu thaa-hi-buu-na ila...

Is the road good?
هل الشارع جيد؟
halish-shaa-ri-'u jay-yid?

How long will
it take?
كم ستستغرق الرحلة؟
kam sa-tas-taq-riq ar-rih-la?

أنت تسير بسرعة عالية جداً an-ta ta-sii-ru bi sur-'a 'aa-li-yah jid-dan	You are driving too fast
رخصة قيادتك رجاءً rukh-sa-tu qi-yaa-da-ti-ka ra-jaa-an	Your driving licence please

Petrol is widely available on main roads.

بترول bat-rool	petrol
البنزين الخالي من الرّصاص al-ban-ziin al-khaa-li min ar-ra-saas	unleaded petrol
ديزل dii-zal	diesel

Where is the nearest petrol station?	أين أقرب محطة البنزين؟ ay-na aq-ra-bu ma-hat-ta-tul bin-ziin?
Fill it up, please	إملأه، رجاءً im-la-hu, ra-jaa-an
Please check the oil	رجاءً افحص الزيت ra-jaa-an, if-has az-zay-t

Driving and petrol

51

| Can I pay by credit card? | هل من الممكن أن أدفع بطاقة الائتمان؟ |
| | hal mi-nal mum-kin an ad-fa'a bi-bi-taa-qah al-i-ti-maa-n? |

YOU MAY HEAR...

ليس لدينا...	We have no...
lay-sa la-day-naa...	
أنت تحتاج إلى زيت	You need oil
an-ta tah-taa-ju ilaa zayt	
أنت تحتاج إلى ماء	You need water
an-ta tah-taa-ju ilaa maa	
أنت تحتاج إلى هواء	You need air
an-ta tah-taa-ju ilaa ha-waa	

Driving

Breakdown

. . . .

If you break down on the motorway, go to the nearest service station and ask for help. It is normal to ask other road users for help and they are usually more than happy to assist.

| My car has broken down | تعطلت سيارتي |
| | ta-'at-ta-lat say-yaa-ra-tii |

Can you help me?	هل تستطيع أن تساعدني؟
	hal-tas-ta-tii-'u an
	tu-saa-'i-da-nii?

| I've run out of petrol | انتهى البترول عندي |
| | in-ta-hal bat-roo-lu 'in-dii |

| I have a flat tyre | عندي إطار فارغ |
| | 'in-dii i-taar faa-riq |

Where is the nearest garage? (repair shop)	أين أقرب ورشة لتصليح السيارات؟
	ay-na aq-rab war-sha li-tas-liih
	as-say-yaa-raat?

| Can you repair it? | هل يمكنك تصليحها؟ |
| | hal-yum-ki-nu-ka tas-lii-hu-haa? |

| How long will it take? | كم من الوقت ستأخذ؟ |
| | kam minal waq-ti sa-ta-khu-th? |

| How much will it cost? | كم ستكلف من المال؟ |
| | kam sa-tu-kal-lif minal maal? |

Car parts

. . . .

Local garages are able to repair cars very quickly.
Repairs are carried out in industrial zones called
si-naa-'iy-yah, which are located in the industrial
estates of towns.

...doesn't work	لا تعمل ...	
	... laa ta'-mal	
Where is the repair shop?	أين ورشة التصليح؟	
	ay-na war-shat at-tas-liih?	
accelerator	المعجّل	al-mu-'aj-jil
alternator	المولد الكهربائي	al-mu-wal-lid al-kah-ru-baa-I
battery	البطارية	al-bat-taa-riya
brakes	الكابحات	al-kaa-bi-haat
choke	الشراقة	ash-shar-raa-qa
clutch	الفاصل	al-faa-sil
engine	المحرّك	al-mu-har-rik
exhaust pipe	أنبوب العادم	un-buub al-'aa-dim
fuse	المصهر	al-mis-har
gears	التروس	at-tu-ruus

54

handbrake	كابح يدوي	kaa-bih ya-da-wi
headlights	الأضواء العلوية	al-ad-waa al-'ul-wiy-yah
ignition	الإيقاد	al-ii-qaad
ignition key	مفتاح الإشتعال	mif-taah al-ish-ti-'aal
indicator	المؤشر	al-mu-ash-shir
lock	القفل	al-qifl
radiator	رادياتور/مبرد المحرك	raad-yaa-tor/ mu-ba-rid al-mu-har-rik
reverse gear	الترس العكسي	at-turs al-'ak-si
seat belt	حزام المقعد	hi-zaam al-miq-'ad
spark plug	شمعة القدح	sham-'atul-qad-h
steering wheel	دولاب القيادة	duu-laab al-qi-yaa-da
tyre	الإطار	al-i-taar
wheel	العجلة	al-'a-ja-la
windscreen	الزجاجة الأمامية	az-zu-jaa-ja al-amaa-miy-ya
windscreen wiper	ماسحة الزجاجة الأمامية	maa-si-hat az-zu-jaa-ja al-amaa-miy-ya

Staying somewhere

Hotel (booking)

Hotels are rated from 1 to 5 stars, although unstarred hotels also exist. In tourist areas it is easy to find a hotel or guesthouse. Breakfast will probably not be included in the room price.

We would like to book a single room	نودّ أن نحجز غرفة لشخص na-wad-du an nah-ji-za qur-fa li-shakhs
We would like to book a double room	نودّ أن نحجز غرفة لشخصين na-wad-du an nah-ji-za qur-fa li-shakh-sayn
For how many nights?	لكم ليلة؟ li-kam lay-lah?

for one night	للیلة واحدة	
	li-lay-lah waa-hi-da	
two nights	لیلتین	
	li-lay-la-tayn	
one week	لأسبوع	
	li-us-buu'	
Is there a hotel nearby?	هل هناك فندق قریب؟	
	hal hu-naa-ka fun-duq qa-riib?	
Is there a guesthouse nearby?	هل هناك بیت للضیوف قریب؟	
	hal hu-naa-ka bayt lit-tu-yuuf qa-riib?	
Do you have a room?	هل لدیك غرفة؟	
	hal la-day-ka qur-fa?	
I'd like...	أرید...	
	u-rii-du...	
a single room	غرفة لشخص	
	qur-fa li-sha-kh-s	
a double room	غرفة لشخصین	
	qur-fa li sha-kh-sayn	

a room for three people	غرفة لـ ٣ أشخاص qur-fa li 3 (tha-laatha) ash-khaas
with shower	بدُش bi-dush
with bath	بحوض الإغتسال bi-haw-d al-iq-ti-saal
How much is it per night?	كم قيمتها في الليلة؟ kam qii-ma-tu-haa fil-lay-lah?
Is breakfast included?	هل هذا يتضمن الفطور؟ hal haa-thaa ya-ta-tham-ma-nu al-if-taar?
I'll be staying...	سأمكث... sa-am-ku-thu...
We'll be staying...	سنمكث... sa-nam-ku-thu...
one night	ليلة واحده lay-la waa-hi-da

two nights	ليلتان
	lay-la-taan

three nights	ثلاث ليالي
	tha-laa-thu la-yaa-lii

Is there anywhere else to stay?	هل هناك أي مكان آخر يمكن المكوث فيه؟
	hal-hu-naa-ka ay-yu ma-kaa-nin aa-khar yum-ki-nul mu-kuu-tha fiih?

YOU MAY HEAR...

اسمك، لو سمحت is-muka law sa-mah-t	Your name, please
جواز السفر، لو سمحت ja-waa-zus-sa-far law sa-mah-t	Your passport, please
المكان ممتلئ al-ma-kaan mum-ta-li	We are full

59

Hotel desk

I have a reservation	عندي حجز 'in-dii haj-z
My name is...	اسمي . . . is-mii...
Have you a different room?	هل لديك غرفة مختلفة؟ hal la-day-ka qur-fa mukh-ta-li-fa?
Where can I park the car?	أين يمكن أن أوقف السيارة؟ ay-na yum-ki-nu an uu-qi-fas-say-yaa-rah?
What time is breakfast?	ما وقت الفطور؟ maa waq-tul-fu-tuur?
What time is dinner?	ما وقت العشاء؟ maa waq-tul-'a-shaa?
The key, please	المفتاح، لو سمحت al-mif-taah law sa-mah-t

60

| Room number... | غرفة رقم... |
| | qur-fa ra-qam... |

| Are there any messages for me? | هل هناك أي رسائل لي؟ |
| | hal hu-naa-ka ay-yu ra-saa-il lii? |

| I'm leaving tomorrow | أنا مغادر غدا |
| | anaa mu-qaa-dir qa-dan |

| Please prepare the bill | حضّر الفاتورة من فضلك |
| | had-dir al-faa-tuu-rah min fad-lak |

Camping

. . . .

Due to the weather, camping is not a particularly popular activity. There are no camp sites like the ones that can be found in the West. You might, however, find yourself camping in the desert of one of the gulf countries for couple of days. It is unlikely that you will see the word 'showers' anywhere. The word 'toilets' '**ham-maa-maat**' is sufficient.

مخيم mu-khay-yam	camp site
ماء للشرب maa lish-shurb	drinking water
الأدشاش al-ad-shaa-sh	showers
مكتب mak-tab	office
الإستقبال al-is-tiq-baal	reception
خيمة	tent

Where is the camp site?	أين المخيم؟ ay-nal mu-khay-yam?
How much is it per night?	كم سعره بالليلة؟ kam si'-ru-hu bil-lay-la?
We want to stay...	نود أن نبقى ... na-wad-du an nab-qaa...
one night	ليلة واحده lay-latun waa-hi-da
two nights	ليلتان lay-la-taan
one week	أسبوع واحد us-buu-'un waa-hid

Where is/are the...?	أين الـ...؟ ay-na al...?
toilets	حمامات ham-maa-maat
showers	الأدشاش al-ad-shaa-sh
drinking water	ماء للشرب maa lish-shurb

YOU MAY HEAR...

المكان ممتلئ al-ma-kaan mum-ta-li	We are full

Self-catering

. . . .

Can you give us an extra set of keys?	هل يمكن أن تعطينا مجموعة إضافيّة من المفاتيح؟ hal yum-kin an tu'-ti-naa maj-muu-'a i-thaa-fiy-ya min al-ma-faa-tiih?

Who do we contact if there are problems?	من نتّصل به إذا كان هناك مشاكل؟ man nat-ta-si-lu bi-hi i-thaa kaa-na hu-naa-ka ma-shaa-kil?
Is there always hot water?	هل هناك ماء ساخن دائماً؟ hal-hu-naa-ka maa-un saa-khin?
Where is the nearest supermarket?	أين أقرب سوبر ماركت؟ ay-na aq-ra-bu su-per-mar-kit?
Where do we leave the rubbish?	أين نترك القمامة؟ ay-na nat-ru-kul qu-maa-mah?

> **Sightseeing and tourist office** (p 81)

Shopping

Shopping phrases

Shops are generally open from 9 am to well after midnight, seven days a week. Some shops close between 12 and 4 pm due to the warm weather, and for siestas. You may also find some shops are closed at prayer times for about 10 minutes. Most towns have a farmers' market **bazar** once a week. At these, good-natured haggling and bargaining is normal: offer half to two-thirds of the asking price, then settle on a price somewhere in between. If you are still not happy with the price, you may just say so and stop the haggling.

A أريد شراء ثوبا أزرق

u-rii-du shi-raa-a thaw-ban az-raq

I would like to buy that blue dress

B ما مقاسك؟

maa ma-qaa-su-ka

What is your size?

A المقاس 40

al-ma-qaas 40

Size 40

Where are the shops?	أين المحلات؟	ay-nal ma-hal-laat?
I'm looking for...	أنا أبحث عن...	anaa ab-ha-thu 'an...
Where is the nearest...?	أين أقرب...؟	ayna aq-rabu...?
Where is the nearest baker's?	أين أقرب خبّاز؟	ayna aq-ra-bu khab-baaz?

66

Where is the bazaar?	أين السّوق؟ aynas-suuq?
Is it open?	هل هو مفتوح؟ hal hu-wa maf-tuuh?
When does it close?	متى يغلق؟ ma-taa yaq-liq?
Can I take that one?	هل يمكن أن آخذ هذا؟١ hal yum-ki-nu an aa-khu-tha haa-thaa?
How much is it?	بكمّ هو؟ bi-kam hu-wa?
It's too expensive	إنه غالي جدّ in-na-hu qaa-lin jid-dan
I don't want it	لا أريده laa u-rii-duh

Shops

• • • • • • • • • • • • • • • • • • • •

Where is the...?	أين...؟	ayna...?
baker's	الخبّاز	al-khab-baaz
bookshop	المكتبة	al-mak-ta-ba
butcher's	الجزّار	al-Jaz-zaar
cake shop	محلّ الكعك	ma-hal-lul ka'k
clothes shop	محلّ الملابس	ma-hal-lul ma-laa-bis
gift/souvenir shop	هدايا/تذكارات	ha-daa-yaa/ ti-th-kaa-raat
greengrocer's	الخضريّ	al-khu-tha-ri
grocer's	البقّال	al-baq-qaal
hairdresser's	الحلاق	al-hal-laaq
jeweller's	الصائغ	as-saa-iq
market	السوق	as-suuq
newsagent's	بائع الصحف	baa-i' as-su-huf
optician's	صانع النظّارات	saa-ni' an-nath-thaa-raat
pharmacy	الصيدليّة	as-say-da-li-yah
shoe shop	محلّ الحذاء	ma-hal-lul hi-thaa
shop	المحلّ	al-ma-hal
shopping centre	المركز التجاريّ	al-mar-kaz at-ti-jaari

spice/herb shop	محلّ التوابل/ الأعشاب	ma-hal at-ta-waa-bil/al-a'-shaab
stationer's	المكتبة	al-mak-ta-ba
supermarket	سوبر ماركت	su-bar mar-kit
tobacconist's	بائع التّبغ	baa-l' at-tab-q
toy shop	محلّ اللّعب	ma-halul la'ib

Food (general)

• •

You can buy most of these from a supermarket.

biscuits	البسكويتات	al-bas-ka-wii-taat
bread	الخبز	al-khubz
butter	الزّبدة	az-zub-da
cakes	الكعك	al-ka'k
cheese	الجبن	al-jub-n
chicken	الدّجاج	ad-da-jaa-j
chocolate	الشّوكولاتة	ash-shu-ku-laa-ta
coffee	القهوة	al-qah-wa
coffee (instant)	قهوة	qah-wa (Nescafé® nes-ka-fe)
crisps	شرائح البطاطس	sha-raa-ih al-ba-taa-tis
egg	بيضة	bay-da
fish	سمك	sa-mak

flour	دقيق	da-qii-q
honey	عسل	'a-sal
jam	مربى	mu-rab-baa
margarine	زبدة	zub-da
marmalade	مربى	mu-rab-baa
milk	لبن/حليب	la-ban/ha-liib
olive oil	زيت الزيتون	zay-tuz-zay-tuun
orange juice	عصير البرتقال	'a-sii-rul bur-tu-qaal
pasta	المكرونة	al-ma-ka-roo-na
pepper (seasoning)	الفلفل (التتبيل)	al-fil-fil (at-tat-biil)
rice	الأرز	al-aruz
salt	الملح	al-mal-h
stock cubes	المرق	al-ma-ra-q
sugar	السكر	as-suk-kar
tea	الشاي	ash-shaa-y
vinegar	الخل	al-khal
yoghurt	الزبادي	az-za-baa-dii

Food (fruit and veg)

· ·

| apples | التفاح | at-tuf-faah |
| apricots | المشمش | al-mish-mish |

> **Measurements and quantities** (p 133)

aubergine	الباذِنْجان	al-baa-thin-jaan
bananas	المَوْز	al-mawz
cabbage	الكُرُنب	al-kar-nab
carrots	الجَزَر	al-ja-zar
cauliflower	القَرْنَبيط	al-qar-na-biid
cherries	الكَرَز	al-ka-raz
courgettes	الكوسا	al-kuu-saa
cucumber	الخِيار	al-kha-yaar
dates	التَمْر	at-tam-r
figs	التّين	at-tiin
garlic	الثّوم	ath-thawm
grapefruit	الجريبفروت	al-grape-fruut
grapes	العِنَب	al-'i-nab
green beans	الفاصوليا الخَضْراء	al-faa-suu-liy-yah al-khad-raa
lemon	اللّيْمون	al-lay-muun
lettuce	الخَسّ	al-khas
melon	الشَّمّام	ash-sham-maam
mushrooms	عيش الغُراب	'esh al-quraab
nectarines	الخَوْخ	al-khuu-kh
onions	البَصَل	al-ba-sal
oranges	البُرتقال	al-bur-tu-qaal
peaches	الخَوْخ	al-khuu-kh
pears	الكُمَّثْرى	al-kum-mith-raa
peas	البِسِلّة	al-ba-sil-lah
peppers	الفُلْفُل	al-fil-fil

pineapple	الأناناس	al-ana-naas
plums	البرقوق	al-bar-quuq
pomegranate	الرمان	ar-rum-maan
potatoes	البطاطس	al-ba-taa-tis
sour-cherries	الكرز الحمضي	al-ka-raz al-him-thi
spinach	السبانخ	as-sa-baa-nikh
strawberries	الفراولة	al-fa-raa-wila
tomatoes	الطماطم	at-ta-maa-tim
watermelon	البطيخ	al-bat-tiikh

Clothes

European sizes are the most commonly used,
however, due to some products being imported
from various parts of the world, other size guides
may be found in some places.

| women's sizes | | men's suit sizes | | shoe sizes | | | |
UK	EU	UK	EU	UK	EU	UK	EU
10	40	36	46	2	35	7	41
12	42	38	48	3	36	8	42
14	44	40	50	4	37	9	43
16	46	42	52	5	38	10	44
18	48	44	54	6	39	11	45
20	50	46	56				

هل يمكن أن أقيس هذا؟

hal yum-kinu an a-qii-sa haa-thaa

Can I try this one on?

نعم، بالطبع، يمكن أن تقيسه هنا

na'am, bit-tab', yum-kinu an ta-qii-sa hu hu-naa

Yes, of course, you can try it on in here

هل عندك هذا في الصغير

hal 'in-da-ka haa-thaa fis-sa-qiir

Do you have this one in a small size?

لا، غير موجود   نعم، موجود

laa, qayr maw-juud   na-'am, maw-juud

No, we don't.   Yes, we do.

Small	صغير	sa-qiir
Medium	وسط	wa-sat
Large	كبير	ka-biir

73

Is it real leather?	هل هذا من جلد حقيقي؟
	hal haa-thaa min jild ha-qii-qii?

Do you have this one in other colours?	هل لديك هذا بلون آخر؟
	hal la-day-ka haa-thaa bi-lawn aa-khar?

It's too expensive	إنه غالي جدا
	in-na-hu qaa-li jid-dan

It's too big	إنه كبير جدا
	in-na-hu ka-biir jid-dan

It's too small	إنه صغير جدا
	in-na-hu sa-qiir jid-dan

No thanks, I don't want it	لا شكرا، لا أريده
	laa shuk-ran, laa u-rii-duh

Clothes (articles)

. . . .

cotton	القطن	al-qutn
leather	الجلد	al-jild

silk	الحرير	al-ha-riir
wool	الصوف	as-suuf
coat	المعطف	al-mi'-taf
dress	اللباس	al-li-baas
hat	القبعة	al-qub-ba-'a
jacket	السترة	as-sut-rah
knickers	الكلسون	al-kal-soon
sandals	الصنادل	as-sin-daal
shirt	القميص	al-qa-miis
shorts	سروال قصير	sir-waal qa-siir
skirt	التنورة	at-tan-nuu-ra
socks	الجوارب	al-ja-waa-rib
swimsuit	كسوة السباحة	kis-wat si-baa-ha
t-shirt	الفانيلة	al-faa-nil-la
trousers	البنطلون	al-ban-ta-loon
underpants	الملابس الداخلية	al-ma-laa-bis ad-daa-khi-liy-yah

Maps and guides

. . . .

Unfortunately it is very difficult to find functional, well-designed maps in most Arab countries. The local tourist information office will usually be able to direct you. The word for map is kha-rii-ta.

Where can I buy a map?	أين يمكن لي أن أشتري خارطة؟ ay-na yum-kinu lii an ash-ta-ri-ya khaa-ri-ta?
Do you have a road map?	هل لديك خارطة طريق؟ hal la-day-ka khaa-ri-da-tu da-riiq?
Do you have a town plan?	هل لديك خارطة القرية؟ hal la-day-ka khaa-ri-da-tul-qar-yah?
Do you have a leaflet in English?	هل لديك منشورة hal la-day-ka man-shuu-rah bil in-gi-lii-ziy-yah
Do you have a guidebook in English?	دليل بالإنجليزية؟ hal la-day-ka da-liil bil in-gi-lii-ziy-yah?
Can you show me where ... is on the map?	تستطيع أن تريني مكان ... على الخارطة؟ tas-ta-dii' an tu-ri-nii ma-kaa-na ... 'a-laal-khaa-ri-da?

> **Asking the way** (p 30)

| Where can I buy a newspaper? | أين أستطيع شراء جريدة؟ |
| | ay-na as-ta-dii-'u shi-raa ja-rii-dah? |

| Have you any newspapers in English? | هل لديك أي جرائد انجليزية؟ |
| | hal la-day-ka ay-yu ja-raa-id in-gil-lii-ziy-yah? |

Post office

Post offices are usually open six days a week, being closed on Fridays.

البريد الجوي al-ba-riid al-jaw-wi	airmail
في الخارج fillkhaa-rij	overseas
داخل البلاد daa-khil al-bil-laad	inland
محلّي ma-hal-lii	local
الرسالة ar-ra-saa-il	letter
البطاقة البريدية al-bi-taa-qa al-ba-rii-diy-yah	postcard
الطوابع at-ta-waa-bi'	stamps

Where is the post office?	أين مكتب البريد؟ ay-na mak-ta-bul-ba-riid?
Where can I buy stamps?	أين أشتري الطوابع؟ ay-na ash-ta-rii ad-da-waa-bi'?
five stamps	خمسة طوابع kham-su da-waa-bi'
10 stamps	عشرة طوابع 'ash-ra-tu da-waa-bi'
for postcards	للبطاقات البريدية lil-bi-taa-qaat al ba-rii-diy-yah
for letters	للرسائل lir-ra-saa-il
to Britain	إلى بريطانيا ilaa bri-taa-ni-yaa
to America	إلى أمريكا ilaa am-rii-kaa
to Australia	إلى أستراليا ilaa us-tu-raa-li-yaa

| to Canada | الى كندا |
| | ilaa kanada |

Photos

. . . .

| colour film | فلم ملون |
| | fi-lim mu-law-wan |

| Where is a photographic shop? | أين دكان التصوير؟ |
| | ay-na duk-kaa-nut-tas-wiir? |

| I need a film for this camera | أنا بحاجة إلى فلم لهذه الكاميرا |
| | ana bi-haa-ja ilaa fi-lim li haa-thi-hii al-kaa-mi-ra |

| I need a memory card for this camera | أنا بحاجة لبطاقة ذاكرة لهذه الكامرا |
| | ana bi-haa-ja ilaa bi-taa-qat thaa-ki-ra li haa-thi-hii al-kaa-mi-ra |

| I need batteries for this | أنا بحاجة إلى بطاريات لهذه |
| | ana bi-haa-ja ilaa bat-taa-riy-yaat li-haa-thi-hi |

79

| I'd like these films developed | أنا أودّ أن أحمض هذه الأفلام |
| | anaa a-wad-du an u-ham-mida haa-thi-hii al af-laam |

| How long will it take? | كم يأخذ هذا؟ |
| | kam ya-khu-thu haa-thaa? |

| How much will it cost? | كم ثمنها؟ |
| | kam tha-ma-nu-haa? |

Leisure

Sightseeing and tourist office

Tourist offices provide lists of places to stay. In some countries like Egypt you will also find maps and leaflets describing local attractions.

استعلامات is-ti'-laa-maat	information
المكتب السياحي a-mak-tab as-si-yaa-hii	tourist office
المتحف al-mit-haf	museum
المعرض الفني al-ma'-rad al-fan-nii	art gallery
مسجد mas-jid	mosque
المنظمة الجولة al-jaw-la al-mu-na-tha-ma	guided tour
التذاكر at-ta-thaa-kir	tickets
الحمام/مرحاض al-ham-maam/mir-haa-th	toilet

Where is the tourist office?	اين المكتب السياحي؟ ay-nal mak-tab as-si-yaa-hi?
What can we visit in the area?	ما الذي يمكننا زيارته في المنطقة؟ mal-la-thii yum-ki-nu-naa zi-yaa-ra-tu-hu fil-man-ti-qa?
Have you got details in English?	هل لديك التفاصيل باللغة الإنجليزية؟ hal la-day-ka at-ta-faa-siil bil-lu-qal-in-gi-lii-ziy-yah?
Are there any excursions?	هل هناك أيّ نزهات؟ hal hu-naa-ka ay-yu nu-zu-haat?
When does it leave?	متى ستقلع؟ ma-taa sa-tuq-li'?
When does it get back?	متى ستعود؟ ma-taa sa-ta-'uud?

> **Maps and guides** (p 75)

Entertainment

. . . .

What is there to do in the evenings?

ماذا هناك للقيام به في أمسيات ؟

ma-thaa hu-naa-ka lil-qi-yaam bi-hi fil-um-siy-yaat?

We would like to go to a disco

نحن نودّ أن نذهب إلى دسكو

nah-nu na-wad-du an nath-ha-ba ilad-disko

Is there anywhere we can go to hear live music?

هل هناك أي مكان يمكن أن نذهبه لنسمع موسيقى حيّة؟

hal hu-naaka ay-yu ma-kaan yum-ki-nu an nath-ha-ba-hu li-sa-maa-I mu-sii-qaa hay-ya?

Is there anywhere we can go to see belly-dancing?

هل هناك أيّ مكان يمكن أن نذهب لرؤية الرقص الشرقي؟

hal hu-naa-ka ay-yu ma-kaan yum-ki-nu an nath-ha-ba li-ru-yat ar-raq-sa ash-sharqii?

Is there any entertainment for children?

هل هناك أيّ ترفيه للأطفال؟

hal-hu-naa-ka ay-yu tar-fiih lil-at-faal?

83

Leisure/beach

. . . .

شاطئ	shaa-ti	beach
خطر	kha-tar	danger
أدشاش	ad-shaa-sh	showers

Are there any good beaches around here?

هل هناك أيّ شواطئ جيدة في هذه النواحي؟

hal hu-naa-ka ay-yu sha-waa-ti jay-yi-da fil haa-thi-hin-na-waa-hii?

Is there a bus to the beach?

هل هناك حافلة الى الشاطئ؟

hal hu-naa-ka haa-fila ilash-shaa-ti?

Is there a shared taxi to the beach?

هل هناك سيارة أجرة جماعية للشاطئ؟

hal hu-naa-ka say-yaa-rat uj-rah ja-maa-'iy-yah ilash-shaa-ti?

Can we go windsurfing?

هلّ بالإمكان أن نذهب لركوب الأمواج ؟

hal bil-im-kaa-ni an nath-ha-ba li-ru-kuu-bil am-waaj?

Please go away!	من فضلك اتركني!
	min fad-lak ut-ruk-nii!

Music

. . . .

Is there anywhere we can go to hear Arabic music?	هل هناك أي مكان يمكن أن نذهب لسماع موسيقى عربية؟
	hal hu-naa-ka ay-yu ma-kaan yum-ki-nu an nath-ha-ba li-sa-maa-'i mu-sii-qaa 'a-ra-biy-ya?

Are there any concerts?	هل هناك أيّ حفلات موسيقية؟
	hal hu-naa-ka ay-yu ha-fa-laat muu-sii-qiy-yah?

Where can I get tickets?	أين أحصل على التذاكر؟
	ay-na ah-su-lu alat-ta-thaa-kir?

Where can I hear some classical music?	أين يمكن أن أسمع بعض الموسيقى الكلاسيكية
	ay-na yum-ki-nu an as-ma-'a ba'-thal-muu-sii-qaa al-ka-laa-sii-kiy-yah

> **Making friends** (p 24)

85

| Where can I hear some jazz? | أين يمكن أن أسمع بعض موسيقى الجاز؟ |

ay-na yum-ki-nu an as-ma-'a ba'-thal-muu-sii-qaa al-jaaz?

Cinema

| سينما si-ni-ma | cinema |
| عرض 'ar-th | screening |

| What's on at the cinema? | ماذا في السينما؟ |

maa-thaa fis-si-ni-maa?

| What time does the film start? | أيّ وقت يبدأ الفلم؟ |

fii ay-yi waq-tin yab-da-ul filim?

| How much are the tickets? | ما قيمة التذاكر؟ |

maa qii-ma-tut-ta-thaa-kir?

| Two for the (give name and time of performance) showing | إثنان لعرض... |

ith-naan li-'ar-dth (...)

لعرض ... ليس لدينا تذاكر متبقية li-'ard ... lay-sa la-day-naa ta-thaa-kir mu-ta-baq-qi-yah	We have no tickets for the ... screening

Mosque

· ·

Women should have their head covered and both men and women should avoid wearing shorts. You will have to leave your shoes at the entrance. Prayers take place five times a day and it is best to wait until these have finished before entering.

مسجد mas-jid	mosque
مسلم mus-lim	Muslim
مسيحي ma-sii-hi	Christian
حذاء hi-thaa	shoes
ممنوع التصوير mam-nuu' at-tas-wiir	no photos
ممنوع التصوير mam-nuu' at-tas-wiir	no videos

| I'd like to see the mosque | أنا أودّ أن أرى المسجد |
| | anaa a-wad-du an a-raal mas-jid |

When can we see the mosque?	متى بالإمكان أن نرى المسجد؟
	ma-taa bil-im-kaa-ni an na-raa
	al mas-jid?

| Where is the mosque? | أين المسجد؟ |
| | ay-nal mas-jid? |

Television

Most Arab countries have state channels which broadcast in Arabic, with films shown in the original language and subtitled. Besides that, other channels broadcast in English for the English speaking viewers and you will find news in English, and Western films. Most hotels and bars have satellite TV.

جهاز التحكّم عن بعد ji-haaz at-ta-hak-kum min bu'-d	remote control
الأخبار al-akh-baar	news
للتشغيل lit-tash-qiil	to switch on
للإطفاء lil-it-faa	to switch off
رسوم متحركة ru-suum mu-ta-har-rika	cartoons

Where is the television?

أين التلفزيون؟
ay-nal ti-li-fiz-yoon?

How do I switch on the television?

كيف أشغّل التلفزيون؟
kay-fa u-sh-'ilu at-ti-li-fiz-yoon?

What's on television?

ماذا يعرض على التلفزيون؟
maa-thaa yu'-radu 'a-lat-tilifiz-yoon?

Are there any channels in English?

هل هناك أيّ قنوات باللغة الإنجليزية؟
hal hu-naa-ka ay-yu qa-na-waat bil-luqal in-gi-lii-ziy-yah?

Are there any children's programmes?	هل هناك أيّ برامج للأطفال؟
	hal hu-naa-ka ay-yu ba-raa-mij lil-at-faal?
When is the football on?	متى تكون كرة القدم الأخبار على الشاشة؟
	ma-taa ta-kuu-nu ku-rat al-qa-dam 'a-lash-shaa-shah?
When is the news on?	متى تكون الأخبار على الشاشة؟
	ma-taa ta-kuu-nu al-akh-baar 'a-lash-shaa-shah?

Sport

Where can we play tennis?	أين يمكننا أن نلعب التنس؟
	ay-na yum-ki-nu-naa an nal-'a-ba at-ta-nis?
Where can we play golf?	أين يمكننا أن نلعب جولف؟
	ay-na yum-ki-nu-naa an nal-'a-ba golf?
Where can we play football?	أين يمكننا أن نلعب كرة القدم؟
	ay-na yum-ki-nu-naa an nal-'a-ba ku-rat al qa-dam?

Can we play tennis?	هلّ بالإمكان أن نلعب التنس؟	hal bi-im-kaa-ni-naa an nal-'a-ba at-ta-nis?
Can we play golf?	هلّ بالإمكان أن نلعب جولف؟	hal bi-im-kaa-ni-naa an nal-'a-ba golf?
Can we hire rackets?	هلّ بالإمكان أن نستأجر المضارب؟	hal bil-im-kaani an nas-ta-ji-ra al-ma-thaa-rib?
Can we hire golf clubs?	هلّ بالإمكان أن نستأجر عصى الجولف؟	hal bil-im-kaani an nas-ta-ji-ra a-saal-golf?
How much is it per hour?	كم سعره بالسّاعة؟	kam si'-ru-hu bis-saa'ah?
Can we watch a football match?	هلّ بالإمكان أن نشاهد مباراة كرة القدم؟	hal bil-im-kaa-ni an nu-shaa-hida mu-baa-raat ku-rat al-qa-dam?

| Where can we get tickets? | أين نحصل على التذاكر؟ |
| | ay-na nah-si-lu 'a-laat-ta-thaa-kir? |

| How do we get to the stadium? | كيف نصل إلى الملعب؟ |
| | kay-fa na-si-lu ilal-mal-'ab? |

Turkish baths

. . . .

Turkish baths are commonly known and available in all Arab countries. A wide variety of treatments and facilities such as saunas and Turkish baths are on offer, and they are easy to find in most hotels in big cities. There are separate times or days for men and women. You are given a couple of towels and wooden bath clogs, and shown to the changing room to undress. Wearing a towel (or swimming costume if the bath-house is mixed) you are shown to a cubicle in the steamy marble washroom. Here, buckets of hot water are poured over you, before you lie on a circular hot marble slab and an attendant rubs your skin with a coarse cloth until your skin glows. You will be finished off with a rinse and a massage.

	Turkish baths
الحمَّامات التركية al-ham-maa-maat at-tur-kiy-yah	Turkish baths
الرجال ar-ri-jaal	men
النساء an-ni-saa	women
حار haar	hot
بارد baa-rid	cold
الصابون as-saa-buun	soap
المنشفة al-min-sha-fa	towel
الليفة al-lii-fa	loofah
نعال الحمَّام ni-'aal-ul-ham-maam	bath clogs
قفاز الفرك الخشن quf-faaz al-fark al-kha-shin	coarse rubbing-glove

Where are the baths?	أين الحمَّامات؟ ay-nal ham-maa-maat?	
Where do I undress?	أين أنزع الملابس؟ ay-na an-zi-'ul ma-laa-bis?	

Is the hamam only for women or is it mixed?	هل الحمام للنساء فقط أم مختلط؟ hal al-ham-maa-mu lin-ni-saa fa-qat am mukh-ta-lad?
I would like a massage	أريد تدليك u-rii-du tad-liik
Where is the steam room?	أين غرفة البخار؟ ay-na qur-fa-tul bu-khaar?

Walking

Are there any guided walks?	هل هناك جولات مع دليل؟ hal hu-naa-ka jaw lat ma da lil?
Do you have a guide to local walks?	هل لديك دليل إلى أماكن التجوّل المحلي؟ hal la-day-ka da-liil ilaa amaa-kin at-ta-jaw-wul al ma-hal-li?

How many kilometres is the walk?	كم عدد كيلومترات الجولة؟ kam 'a-dad kilo-mit-raat al-jaw-lah?
How long will it take?	كم من الوقت يأخذ؟ kam min al-waq-ti ya-khuth?
Is it very steep?	هل هو منحدر جدا؟ hal hu-wa mun-ha-dir jid-dan?
I'd like to go climbing	أودّ أن أذهب للتسلّق awad-du an ath-ha-ba lit-ta-sal-luq

> **Maps and guides** (p 75)

Communications

Telephone and mobile

. . . .

If you plan to make international calls, a phonecard
is the most convenient way of paying for them. To
phone Egypt, the international code is oo 20 plus
the Egyptian area code followed by the number.
Please check the international access code for your
destination.

عملة الهاتف 'um-lat al-haa-tif	phone token
بطاقة الهاتف bi-taa-qat al-haa-tif	phonecard
دليل الهاتف da-liil al-haa-tif	telephone directory
(الدفع العكسي) كلكت ad-daf' al-'ak-si	reverse charges (collect)
رمز الإتصال الهاتفي ramz al-it-ti-saal al-haa-ti-fi	dialling code

مرحبا...

marhaba...

Hello

مرحبا، هذا... أودّ أن أتكلّم مع...

mar-haba, haa-thaa... awad-du an ata-kal-lama ma'a...

Hello, this is... I would like to speak to...

ثانية واحدة

thaa-ni-yah waa-hi-da

Just a second

I want to make a phone call	أريد إجراء مكالمة هاتفية
	urii-du ij ra'a mu-kaa-la-mah haa-ti-fiy-yah
I want to phone the UK	أريد أن أتصل بالمملكة المتحدة
	urii-du an at-tasila bil-mam-laka al-mut-ta-hi-da
I want to phone Canada	أريد أن أتصل بكندا
	urii-du an at-tasila bikanada
I want to phone Australia	أريد أن اتصل بأستراليا
	urii-du an at-tasila biustralia

| I want to phone the USA | أريد أن أتصل بأمريكا |
| | urii-du an at-tasila biamerica |

| An outside line, please | خط خارجي، رجاء |
| | khat khaa-ri-ji, ra-jaa-an |

| Where can I buy a phonecard? | أين أشتري بطاقة الهاتف؟ |
| | ay-na ash-ta-rii bi-taa-qat-tul-haa-tif? |

| Please write the phone number down | رجاء إكتب رقم الهاتف |
| | ra-jaa-an uk-tub ra-qam al-haa-tif |

| Do you have a mobile phone? | هل لديك هاتف جوّال؟ |
| | hal la-day-ka haa-tif jaw-waal? |

| Can I speak to... | هل من الممكن أن أتكلم مع... |
| | hal minal-mum-kin an ata-kal-lama ma-'a... |

| This is... | هذا... |
| | haa-thaa... |

| I'll call back later | سأعيد الإتصال لاحقا |
| | sa-u-'ii-du al-it-ti-saa-la laa-hi-qan |

I'll call again tomorrow	سأتصل ثانية غدا sa-at-ta-silu thaa-ni-ya-tan qa-dan

YOU MAY HEAR...

مرحبا mar-haba	Hello
لحظة لو سمحت lah-tha law sa-maht	Please hold on
من المتصل؟ man-nil mut-ta-sil?	Who is calling?
هلّ بالإمكان أن تتصل لاحقا؟ hal bil-im-kaan an tat-ta-sila laa-hi-qan?	Can you call back later?
هلّ تريد ترك رسالة؟ hal tu-rii-du tar-ka ri-saa-lah?	Do you want to leave a message?
الرقم غلط ar-ra-qam qa-lad	Wrong number
جهاز الإجابة الآلي ji-haaz al ija ba al ali	Answering machine

Text messaging

• • • • • • • • • • • • • • • • • • • •

SMS is a very popular communication tool.

I will text you	سأبعث إليك رسالة sa-ab-'a-thu ilay-ka ri-saa-lah
Can you text me?	هلّ بالإمكان أن ترسل إلي رسالة؟ hal bil-im-kaa-ni an tur-sila ilay-ya ri-saa-la?
Did you get my text message?	هل وجدت رسالتي؟ hal wa-jat-ta ri-saa-la-tii?
Can you send me a picture with your mobile?	هل تستطيع أن ترسل إلي صورة بجوالك ؟ hal tas-ta-dii-'u an tur-sila ilay-ya suu-ra-tan bi-jaw-waa-lak?
Hello	مرحبا mar-haba
Hello (to answer the phone)	مرحبا/ألو mar-haba/alo

| See you | أراك لاحقا |
| | araa-ka laa-hi-qan |

| Tomorrow | غدا |
| | qa-dan |

| Please call me | رجاء إتّصل بي |
| | ra-jaa-an it-tasil bii |

| Today | اليوم |
| | al-yawm |

| Too late | متأخر جدا |
| | mu-ta-akhir jid-dan |

| Tonight | الليلة |
| | al-lay-la |

| Text me | راسلني |
| | raa-sil-nii |

| Free to talk? | هل تستطيع الكلام؟ |
| | hal tas-ta-dii-'ul ka-laam? |

| I will call you back later | سأتّصل بك لاحقا |
| | sa-at-ta-si-lu bi-ka laa-hi-qan |

Thanks	شكرا
	shuk-ran

Are you ok?	هل أنت بخير؟
	hal anta bi-khayr?

E-mail

. . . .

Almost every country has its own top-level domain
(TLD) which is the last part of an Internet domain
name. For example, Egypt's is '**.eg**'; Morocco's is
'**.mc**'; and Tunisia's is '**.tn**'). The '**.com**' domain is
used in all the Arab countries.

Do you have	هل لك بريد إلكتروني؟
e-mail?	hal la-ka ba-riid ilik-troo-ni?

My e-mail	عنوان بريدي الإلكتروني...
address is...	'un-waa-nu ba-rii-dii
	al-ilik-trooni...

What is your	ما هو عنوان بريدك الإلكتروني؟
e-mail address?	ma hu-wa 'un-waa-nu
	ba-rii-da-kal ilik-trooni?

| How do you spell it? | كيف تهجيه؟ |
| | kay-fa tu-haj-jiih? |

| All one word | كلها كلمة واحدة |
| | kul-lu-haa ka-li-mah waa-hi-da |

| All lower case | جميعها حروف صغيرة |
| | ja-mii-'u-haa hu-ruuf-sa-qii-ra |

| Can I send an e-mail? | هل وصلك بريدي الإلكتروني؟ |
| | hal wa-sa-la-ka ba-rii-dii al ilik-troo-ni? |

| Did you get my e-mail? | هل وصلك البريد الإلكتروني مني؟ |
| | hal wa-sa-la-ka ba-rii-dii al ilik-troo-ni? |

Internet

. . . .

Most computer terminology tends to be in English.
Internet cafés are widespread and very popular.

home	الصفحة الرئيسية	as-saf-ha ar-ra-ii-siy-yah
username	اسم المستعمل	ismul-mus-takh-dim
to browse	يتصفح	ya ta sa fah
search engine	وسيلة البحث	was ilat el ba hath
password	كلمة السر	ka-li-mat as-sir
contact us	اتّصل بنا	it-tasil bi-naa
back to menu	عد إلى القائمة	'ud ilal-qaa-i-mah
sitemap	خريطة الموقع	kha ritat el maw qi

Are there any
Internet cafés
here?

هل هناك أيّ مقاهي الإنترنت هنا؟
hal hu-naa-ka ay-yu ma-qaa-hii
inter-net hu-naa?

How much is it
to log on for
an hour?

كم سعر الإتّصال بشبكت الانترنت
لساعة؟
kam si'-rul it-ti-saal bi sha-ba-kat
al-inter-net li-saa-'ah?

104

| I would like to print some pages | أودّ أن أطبع بعض الصفحات <br> awad-du an ad-ba-'a <br> ba'-thas-sa-fa-haat |

Fax

. . . .

To send a fax to Egypt, the international code is 00 20 plus the Egyptian area code (e.g. 2) followed by the number.

من min	from
إلى ilaa	to
التأريخ at-taa-riikh	date
صفحات بتضمين هذه... ...sa-fa-haat bi-that-miin haa-thih	...pages including this

| I want to send a fax | أريد إرسال فاكس <br> u-rii-du ir-saa-la fax |

| Do you have a fax? | هل لديك فاكس؟
 hal la-day-ka faa-ks? |

Where can I send a fax?	أين أستطيع أن أرسل فاكسًا؟ ay-na as-ta-dii-'u an ur-si-la fak-san?
How much is it to send a fax?	كم سعر إرسال الفاكس؟ kam si'-ru ir-saa-lil-faa-ks?
What is your fax number?	ما رقم فاكسك؟ maa ra-qa-mu faak-si-ka?
The fax number is...	رقم الفاكس هو... ra-qa-mul-faa-ks hu-wa...

Practicalities

Money

. . . .

Banks are closed on Fridays. The best place to
change money is at a المصرف **Al Masraf** or bureau
de change. If there is no bureau de change around,
jewellery shops can also change money. It is easier
to change cash than traveller's cheques in some
countries, but in more tourist orientated countries
traveller's cheques are not a problem at all. The
Egyptian currency is the Egyptian pound, the
Moroccan currency is the dirham and the Tunisian
currency is the Tunisian dinar.

Where is the nearest bank?	أين أقرب بنك؟ ay-na aq-ra-bu bank?
Where is the nearest bureau de change?	أين أقرب مكتب صرافة؟ ay-na aq-ra-bu mak-tab sar-raa-fah?

| Can I change money here? | هل بالإمكان أن أصرف نقودا هنا؟ |
| | hal bil-im-kaan an as-ri-fa nu-quu-dan hu-naa? |

| What is the exchange rate? | ما سعر الصرف؟ |
| | maa si'-rus-sar-raa-fah? |

| I want to change £50 | أريد صرف ٥٠£ |
| | u-rii-du sar-fa ٥٠£ |

| I want to change traveller's cheques | أريد صرف صكوك المسافرين (فقط في البنوك) |
| | u-rii-du sar-fa su-kuuk al-mu-saa-fi-riin |

Paying

. . . .

Credit cards are becoming more widely accepted.
Service charges are included in restaurants,
bars and cafés, but a tip is still customary. It is,
however, a good idea to have cash on you when
buying things.

الفاتورة al-faa-tuu-ra	bill
الإيصال al-ii-saal	receipt
الفاتورة al-faa-tuu-ra	invoice
نقطة الدفع nuq-dat ad-daf'	cash desk
بطاقة الإئتمان bi-taa-qat al-i-ti-maan	credit card

I'd like to pay now
أودّ أن أدفع الآن
a-wad-du an ad-fa-'a al-aan

How much is it?
كم المبلغ؟
kam al-mab-laq?

Can I pay... ?
هل بالإمكان أن أدفع...
hal bil-im-kaa-ni an ad-fa-'a...

by credit card
بالبطاقة الائتمانية
bil-bitaa-qa al-i-ti-maa-niy-ya

with traveller's cheques
بصكوك المسافرين
bi-su-kuuk al-mu-saa-fi-riin

Can I pay by cheque?
هل بالإمكان أن أدفع بشيك (صك)؟
hal bil-im-kaa-ni an ad-fa-'a shiik (sak)?

| Where do I pay? | أين أدفع؟ |
| | ay-na ad-fa'? |

| Please write down the price | رجاء إكتب السعر |
| | ra-jaa-an uk-tub as-si'r |

| Put it on my bill (in hotel) | ضعه على فاتورتي في (الفندق) |
| | da'-hu 'a-laa faa-tuu-ra-tii (fil-fun-duq) |

| I'd like a receipt, please | أودّ إيصالا، رجاء |
| | a-wad-du ii-saa-lan, ra-jaa-an |

| I think there is a mistake | أعتقد أن هناك خطأ |
| | a'-ta-qi-du an-na hu-naa-ka kha-ta |

| Keep the change | إحتفظ بالباقي |
| | ih-ta-fid bil-baa-qii |

Luggage

. . . .

الحقيبة al-ha-qii-ba	suitcase
حقيبة يدوية ha-qii-ba ya-da-qiy-yah	handbag
الحقيبة al-ha-qii-ba	briefcase
الأمتعة اليدوية al-am-ti-'a al-ya-da-wy-yah	hand luggage
مكتب إيداع الحقائب mak-tab ii-daa' al-ha-qaa-ib	left luggage office
الخزانة al-khaz-nah	locker
العربة al-'a-ra-bah	trolley

My suitcase hasn't arrived	حقيبتي ما وصلت ha-qii-ba-tii maa wa-sa-lat
My suitcase is missing	حقيبتي مفقودة ha-qii-ba-tii maf-quu-dah
My suitcase is damaged	حقيبتي متضرّرة ha-qii-ba-tii mu-ta-dar-ri-rah

> **Train** (p 37) > **Air travel** (p 45)

| Can I leave my suitcase here? | هلّ بالإمكان أن أترك حقيبتي هنا؟ hal bil-im-kaa-ni an at-ru-ka ha-qii-ba-tii hu-naa? |

| Is there a left luggage office? | هل هناك مكتب إيداع الحقائب؟ hal hu-naa-ka mak-tab ii-daa' al-ha-qaa-ib? |

| When does it open? | متى يفتح؟ ma-taa yaf-tah? |

| When does it close? | متى يغلق؟ ma-taa yuq-liq? |

Repairs

دكان تصليح الحذاء duk-kaan tas-liih al-hi-thaa	shoe repair shop
التصليحات بينما تنتظر at-tas-lii-haat bay-na-maa tan-ta-thir	repairs while you wait

Where can I get this repaired?	أين أستطيع أن أصلح هذا؟ ay-na as-ta-dii-'u an u-sal-li-ha haa-thaa?
This is broken	هذا مكسور haa-thaa mak-suur
Can you repair...?	هلّ تستطيع تصليح...؟ hal tas-ta-dii-'u tas-lii-ha...?
my glasses?	نظاراتي؟ nath-thaa-raa-tii?
my camera?	آلة تصويري (كامرتي)؟ aa-lat tas-wii-rii (kee-ma-ra-tii)?
How much will it cost?	كم ستكلّف؟ kam sa-tu-kal-lif?
How long will it take?	كم من الوقت يأخذ؟ kam min al-waq-ti ya-khu-th?

> **Breakdown** (p 52)

Laundry

· ·

مسحوق الغسيل mas-huuq al-qa-siil	washing powder
maq-sa-lah مغسلة	launderette
المنظف الجاف al-mu-na-thif al-jaaf	dry-cleaner's

Where can
I wash
some clothes?

أين أغسل بعض الملابس؟
ay-na aq-si-lu
ba'-thal-ma-laa-nis?

Do you have a
laundry service?

هل لديك خدمة تغسيل الملابس؟
hal la-day-ka khid-mat taq-siil
al-ma-laa-bis?

Where is the
launderette?

أين محل غسيل الملابس؟
ay-na ma-hal qa-siil
al-ma-laa-bis?

Where is the
dry-cleaner's?

أين المنظف الجاف؟
ay-na al-mu-na-thiful-jaaf?

| Can I borrow an iron? | هلّ بإمكاني أن أستعير مكواتك؟ |
| | hal bi-im-kaa-nii an as-ta-'ii-ra mik-waa-tak? |

| لكلّ واحده | per item |
| li-kul-li waa-hi-da | |

Complaints

| This doesn't work | هذا لا يعمل |
| | haa-thaa laa ya'-mal |

| The room is dirty | إنّ الغرفة قذرة |
| | in-nal-qur-fah qa-thi-ra |

| The room is too hot | إنّ الغرفة حارة جدا |
| | in-nal-qur-fah haar-rah jid-dan |

| The room is too cold | إنّ الغرفة بارده جدا |
| | in-nal-qur-fah baa-ri-dah jid-dan |

| I didn't order this | أنا لم أطلب هذا |
| | anaa lam at-lub haa-thaa |

Complaints

| I want to complain | أريد الشكوى |
| | u-rii-dush-shak-waa |

| Please call the manager | رجاء إتصل بالمدير |
| | ra-jaa-an it-ta-sil bil-mu-diir |

| ...out of order | عاطل... |
| | ... 'aa-til |

| toilet | المرحاض |
| | al-mir-haad |

| shower | الدش |
| | ad-dush |

| television | التلفزيون |
| | at-ti-li-fiz-yoon |

Problems

. . . .

Can you help me?	هلّ بإمكانك أن تساعدني؟
	hal bil-im-kaa-ni-ka an
	tu-saa-'i-da-nii?

> **Hotel desk** (p 60)

| I don't speak Arabic | أنا لا أتكلّم اللغة العربية |
| | anaa laa at-ta-kal-la-mu al-lu-qa al-'a-ra-biy-ya |

| Do you speak English? | هل تتكلّم الانجليزية؟ |
| | hal ta-ta-kal-la-mu al-in-gi-lii-ziy-yah? |

| Is there someone who speaks English? | هل هناك من يتكلّم الانجليزية؟ |
| | hal hu-naa-ka man ya-ta-kal-la-mul-in-gi-lii-ziy-ya? |

| I'm lost | أنا تائه |
| | anaa taa-ih |

| I need to go to... | أريد الذهاب إلى... |
| | u-rii-du ath-tha-haa-ba ilaa... |

| the station | المحطة |
| | al-ma-hat-ta |

| my hotel | فندقي |
| | fun-du-qii |

| this address | هذا العنوان |
| | haa-thaa al-'un-waan |

Problems

117

I've missed my train	فَوَّتُّ قِطَارِي faw-wat-tu qi-taa-rii
I've missed my bus	فَوَّتُّ حَافِلَتِي faw-wat-tu haa-fi-la-tii
I've missed my plane	فَوَّتُّ طَائِرَتِي faw-wat-tu taa-i-ra-tii
I've missed the connection	فَوَّتُّ الوَصْلَة faw-wat-tu al-was-la
The coach has left without me	رَحَلَتِ الحَافِلَة بِدُونِني ra-ha-lat haa-fi-la-tii bi-duu-nii
How does this work?	كَيْفَ يَعْمَلُ هَذَا؟ kay-fa ya'-ma-lu haa-thaa?
That man is following me	ذَلِكَ الرَّجُلُ يَتْبَعُنِي thaa-li-kar-ra-ju-lu yat-ba-'u-nii
I have lost my money	فَقَدْتُ مَالِي fa-qat-tu maa-lii

Emergencies

. . . .

الشرطة ash-shur-ta	police
اطفائية it-faa-iy-ya	fire brigade
سيارة الإسعاف say-yaa-rat is-'aaf	ambulance
المستشفى al-mus-tash-faa	hospital
الحوادث و الطوارئ al-ha-waa-dith wat-ta-waa-ri	A&E

Help!   النجده!
an-naj-da!

Fire!   حريق!
ha-riiq!

There's been   هناك حادث
  an accident   hu-naa-ka haa-dith

Please help me   رجاء ساعدني
ra-jaa-an saa-'id-nii

| Please call the police | رجاء إتّصل بالشرطة |
| | ra-jaa-an it-ta-sil bish-shur-ta |

| Please call the fire brigade | رجاء إتّصل بالاطفائية |
| | ra-jaa-an it-ta-sil bi it-faa-iy-yah |

| Someone has been injured | شخص ما أصيب |
| | shakh-sun ma u-siib |

| Where is the police station? | أين مركز الشرطة؟ |
| | ay-na mar-kaz ash-shur-ta? |

| I've been robbed | لقد سرقت |
| | la-qad su-riqt |

| I've been raped | لقد إغتصبت |
| | la-qad iq-tu-sibt |

| I want to speak to a policewoman | أريد الكلام مع شرطية |
| | u-rii-dul-ka-laa-ma ma-'a shur-tiy-ya |

| Someone has stolen... | شخص سرق... |
| | shakh-sun sa-ra-qa... |

Practicalities

I've lost...	فقدت ...	fa-qat-tu...
my money	مالي	maa-lii
my passport	جواز سفري	ja-waa-za sa-fa-rii
my air ticket	تذاكري	ta-thaa-ki-rii
My son is missing	إبني مفقود	ib-nii maf-quud
My daughter is missing	بنتي مفقودة	bin-tii maf-quu-da
His/Her name is...	اسمه/اسمها ...	is-mu-hu/is-mu-haa...
I need a report for my insurance	أحتاج تقريرا لشركة التأمين	ah-taa-ju taq-rii-ran li-sha-ri-kat at-ta-miin

Please call the British Embassy	رجاء إتصل بالسفارة البريطانية ra-jaa-an it-ta-sil bis-sa-faa-rah al-bri-taa-niy-yah
Please call the Canadian Embassy	رجاء إتصل بالسفارةالكندية ra-jaa-an it-ta-sil bis-sa-faa-rah al kanadiyah
Please call the American Embassy	رجاء إتصل بالسفارة الأمريكية ra-jaa-an it-ta-sil bis-sa-faa-rah al-am-rii-kiy-yah
Please call the Australian Embassy	رجاء إتصل بالسفارة الأسترالية ra-jaa-an it-ta-sil bis-sa-faa-rah alustraliah

Health

Pharmacy

· ·

Pharmacies صيدلية (say-da-liy-ya) keep the same hours as other shops. Pharmacists often speak some English.

أين أقرب صيدلية؟
ay-na aq-ra-bu say-da-liy-yah?

Where is the nearest pharmacy?

I need
  something...

أحتاج شيء...
ah-taa-ju shay-an...

for diarrhoea

للإسهال
lil is-haal

for constipation

للإمساك
lil im-saak

for food
  poisoning

للتسمّم الغذائي
lit-ta-sam-mum al-qi-thaa-ii

123

Is it safe for...?	هل هو آمن لـ ...؟ hal hu-wa aa-min li...?	
children	الأطفال al-at-faal	
I am pregnant	أنا حامل anaa haa-mil	
What is the dose?	ما الجرعة؟ mal jur-'ah?	

YOU MAY HEAR...

3 مرات في اليوم 3 mar-raat fil yawm	three times a day
قبل/بعد الغذاء qab-la/ba'-da al-qa-daa	before/after food
مع الغذاء ma-'al qa-daa	with food

Body

. . . .

I have broken...
إنكسرت...
in-ka-sa-rat...

my foot
قدمي
qa-da-mii

my ankle
كاحلي
kaa-hi-lii

my hand
يدي
ya-dii

my arm
ذراعي
thi-raa-'ii

It hurts
تألمني
tu-li-mu-nii

Doctor

. . . .

المستشفى al-mus-tash-faa	hospital
قسم الضحايا qis-muth-tha-haa-yaa	casualty department
الوصفة al-was-fa	prescription
سيارة الإسعاف say-yaa-tu is-'aaf	ambulance

FACE TO FACE

A أشعر بالتوعك
as'ur bi-ta wa' uk
I don't feel right

B هل عندك سخونة؟
hal 'in-da-ka su-khuu-na?
Do you have a temperature?

A لا. عندي ألم هنا
laa. 'in-dii alam hu-naa
No. I have a pain here

I need to see a doctor	أحتاج لرؤية طبيب ah-taa-ju il-ru-ya-ti ta-biib

My son/daughter is ill	إبني مريض/بنتي مريضة
	ib-nii/bin-tii ma-rii-tha

Will he have to go to hospital?	هل عليه أن يذهب إلى المستشفى؟
	hal 'a-lay-hi an yath-ha-ba ilal-mus-tash-faa?

Will she have to go to hospital?	هل يجب عليها أن تذهب إلى المستشفى؟
	hal ya-jibu 'a-lay-ha an tath-ha-ba ilal-mus-tash-faa?

I'm on the Pill	أنا أتناول حبوب منع الحمل
	anaa atanaa-wa-lu hu-buuba man'il-haml

I'm diabetic	أنا مريض بالسكر
	anaa ma-rii-th bis-suk-kar

I need insulin	أحتاج أنسيولين
	ah-taaj in-su-liin

I'm allergic to penicillin	عندي حسّاسية من البنسلين
	'in-dii ha-saa-si-ya min al-bin-si-liin

Doctor

> **Emergencies** (p 119)

Will I have to pay?	هل يجب عليّ أن أدفع؟
	hal ya-ji-bu 'a-lay-ya an ad-fa-'a?
Can you give me a receipt for the insurance?	هلّ بالإمكان أن تعطيني وصل إستلام للتأمين؟
	hal bil-im-kaan an tu'-dii-nii wasl is-ti-laam lit-ta-miin?

Dentist

. . . .

You will have to pay for dental work at the time of treatment, so be sure to ask for a receipt so that you can claim a refund from your holiday insurance. Make sure you choose a clean and well presented dentist.

الحشوة al-ha-sh-wa	filling
التاج at-taaj	crown
أطقم الأسنان at-qumul-as-naan	dentures
الحقن al-hu-qan	injection

| I need to go to a dentist | أحتاج للذهاب إلى طبيب أسنان |
| | ah-taaj lith-tha-haabi ilaa ta-bii-bi as-naan |

| He has toothache | هوعنده وجع أسنان |
| | hu-wa 'in-da-hu wa-ja' as-naan |

| She has toothache | هي عندها وجع أسنان |
| | hi-ya 'in-da-haa wa-ja' as-naan |

| This hurts | هذا يؤلِم |
| | haa-thaa yu-li-mu |

| My filling has come out | حشوة سني خرج |
| | hash-wii kha-raj |

| My crown has come out | تاجي خرج |
| | taaj-jii kha-raj |

| Can you do emergency treatment? | هلّ بالإمكان أن تعمل معالجة مستعجلة؟ |
| | hal bil-im-kaa-ni an ta'-ma-la mu-'aa-la-ja mus-ta'-ji-la? |

129

Different types of travellers

Disabled travellers

Is there a toilet for the disabled?	هل هناك مرحاض للمعوّقين؟ hal hu-naa-ka mir-haad lil-mu-'aw-wa-qiin?
I want a room on the ground floor	أريد غرفة على الطابق الأرضي u-rii-du qur-fa 'a-lat-taabiq al-ar-dii
Can I enter in a wheelchair?	هلّ بالإمكان أن أدخل في كرسي المعوّقين؟ hal bil-im-kaan an ad-khu-la fii kur-siy-yil mu-'aw-wa-qiin?
Is there a lift?	هل هناك مصعد؟ hal hu-naa-ka mis-'ad?

> **Hotel (booking)** (p 56)

| Where is the lift? | أين المصعد؟ |
| | ay-nal mis-'ad? |

| Is there a reduction for the disabled? | هل هناك تخفيض للمعوّقين؟ |
| | hal hu-naa-ka takh-fiid lil mu-'aw-wa-qiin? |

| I am deaf | أنا أصمّ |
| | anaa a-sam |

With kids

| A child's ticket | تذكرة لطفل |
| | that-ka-ra li-tifl |

| He is ... years old | هي عمرها... سنوات |
| | hi-ya 'um-ru-haa ... sa-na-waat |

| She is ... years old | هو عمره ... سنوات |
| | hu-wa 'um-ruhu ... sa-na-waat |

| Is there a reduction for children? | هل هناك تخفيض للأطفال؟ |
| | hal hu-naa-ka takh-fiid lil at-faal? |

Do you have a children's menu?	هل لديكم قائمة أطفال؟ hal la-day-kum qaa-i-ma-tu at-faal?
Is it OK to take children?	هل من الممكن اصطحاب الأطفال؟ hal min-nal mum-kin is-ti-haa-bul at-faal?
Do you have...?	هل عندك...؟ hal 'in-da-ka...?
a high chair	كرسي أطفال kur-si' atfal
a cot	مهد mahd

> **Doctor** (p 126)

Reference

Measurements and quantities

● ●

Liquids السوائل as-sa-waa-il

half a litre of...	نصف لتر	nisf li-tir...
one litre of...	لتر واحد	li-tar waa-hid...
two litres of...	لتران	lit-raan...
a carafe/jug of...	دورق	daw-raq...
a bottle of...	قنينة	qin-nii-nah...
a glass of...	زجاج	zu-jaa-ja...

Weights الأوزان al-aw-zaan

100 grams of...	١٠٠ غرام	100 qa-raam...
half a kilo of...	نصف كيلو	nisf kii-loo...
one kilo of...	كيلو واحد	kii-loo waa-hid...
two kilos of...	كيلوان	kii-loo-waan...

Food الغذاء al-qi-thaa

a slice of...	شريحة	sha-rii-ha...
a portion of...	جزء	juz...
a dozen	دزينة	du-zee-na...
a box/tin of...	صندوق/علبة	sun-duuq/'ul-ba...
a carton of...	كارتون	kar-toon...
a packet of...	حزمة	hiz-ma...
a jar of...	جرة	jar-ra...

Numbers

In Arabic, numbers are followed by the singular, so you would ask for six peach, two tea, seven stamp, etc.

٠	0	صفر	sifr
١	1	واحد	waa-hid
٢	2	إثنان	ith-naan
٣	3	ثلاثة	tha-laa-tha
٤	4	أربعة	ar-ba-'a
٥	5	خمسة	kham-sa
٦	6	ستة	sit-ta
٧	7	سبعة	sab-'a
٨	8	ثمانية	tha-maa-ni-ya

٩	9	تسعة	tis-'a
١٠	10	عشرة	'a-sha-ra
١١	11	أحد عشر	a-ha-da 'a-shar
١٢	12	إثنا عشر	ith-naa 'a-shar
١٣	13	ثلاثة عشر	tha-laa-tha 'a-shar
١٤	14	أربعة عشر	ar-ba-'a-ta 'a-shar
١٥	15	خمسة عشر	kham-sa-ta 'a- shar
١٦	16	ستة عشر	sit-ta-ta 'a-shar
١٧	17	سبعة عشر	sab-'a-ta 'a-shar
١٨	18	ثمانية عشر	tha-maa-niya-ta 'a-shar
١٩	19	تسعة عشر	tis-'a-ta 'a-shar
٢٠	20	عشرون	'ish-ruun
٢١	21	واحد و عشرون	waa-hid wa 'ish-ruun
٢٢	22	إثنان وعشرون	ith-naan wa 'ish-ruun
٣٠	30	ثلاثون	tha-laa-thuun
٤٠	40	أربعون	ar-ba-'uun
٥٠	50	خمسون	kham-suun
٦٠	60	ستون	sit-tuun
٧٠	70	سبعون	sab-'uun
٨٠	80	ثمانون	tha-maa-nuun
٩٠	90	تسعون	tis-'uun
١٠٠	100	مائة	mi-ah
٢٠٠	200	مئتان	mi-a-taan
٣٠٠	300	ثلاث مائة	tha-laa-thu mi-ah
٤٠٠	400	أربع مائة	ar-ba-u mi-ah
٥٠٠	500	خمس مائة	kham-su mi-ah

135

١٬٠٠٠	**1,000**	ألف	alf
٢٬٠٠٠	**2,000**	ألفان	al-faan
٣٬٠٠٠	**3,000**	ثلاث آلاف	tha-laa-thu aa-laaf
١٠٬٠٠٠	**10,000**	عشرة آلاف	ash-ra-tu aa-laaf
١٠٠٬٠٠٠	**100,000**	مائة ألف	mi-a-tu alf
١٬٠٠٠٬٠٠٠	**1,000,000**	مليون	mil-yoon

first	الأول	al-aw-wal
second	الثاني	ath-thaa-nii
third	الثالث	ath-thaa-lith
fourth	الرابع	ar-raa-bi
fifth	الخامس	al-khaa-mis
sixth	السادس	as-saa-dis
seventh	السابع	as-saa-bi'
eighth	الثامن	ath-thaa-min
ninth	التاسع	at-taa-si'
tenth	العاشر	al-'aa-shir

Days and months

· ·

Days
· · · · · ·

Monday	الإثنين	al-ith-nain
Tuesday	الثلاثاء	ath-thu-laa-thaa
Wednesday	الأربعاء	al-ar-bi-'aa
Thursday	الخميس	al-kha-miis
Friday	الجمعة	al-jum-'a
Saturday	السبت	as-sabt
Sunday	الأحد	al-a-had

Months
· · · · · · · · · · ·

January	يناير/كانون الثّاني	ya-naa-yir/kaa-nuun ath-thaa-nii
February	فبراير/شباط	fib-raa-yir/shi-baat
March	مارس/آذار	maa-ris/aa-thaar
April	أبريل/نيسان	ab-riil/nii-saan
May	مايو/أيار	maa-yoo
June	يونيو/حزيران	yuun-yuu/ hu-zay-raan
July	يوليو/تموز	yuul-yuu/ta-muuz
August	أغسطس/آب	a-qus-tus/aab
September	سبتمبر/أيلول	sib-tam-bar/ay-luul

137

October	أكتوبر/تشرين الأول	ak-too-ber/tish-riin al-aw-wal
November	نوفمبر/تشرين الثّاني	noo-fam-ber/tish-riin ath-thaa-nii
December	ديسمبر/كانون الأول	dii-sam-ber/kaa-nuun al-aw-wal

Seasons

spring	الربيع	ar-ra-bii'
summer	الصيف	as-sayf
autumn	الخريف	al-kha-riif
winter	الشتاء	ash-shi-taa

Time

The 24-hour clock is used on timetables, etc.

am (morning) صباحا
sa-baa-han

It's midday الظهر
ath-thuhr

pm (afternoon)	مساءا	ma-saa-an
It's...	انها	in-na-haa
It's one o'clock	انها الساعة الواحدة	in-na-haa as-saa-'ah al waa-hi-da
It's two o'clock	انها الساعة الثانية	in-na-haa as-saa-'ah ath-thaa-ni-ya
What time is it?	كم الساعة؟	kamis-saa-'ah?

الساعة التاسعة as-saa-'atut-taa-si-'a	9.00
الساعة التاسعة و عشر دقائق as-saa-'atut-taa-si-'a wa 'ash-ru da-qaa-iq	9.10

الساعة التاسعة و خمسة عشر دقيقة as-saa-'atut-taa-si-'a wa kham-sa-ta 'ash-ra da-qii-qa	quarter past nine
الساعة التاسعة و نصف as-saa-'atut-taa-si-'a wa nisf	9.30
الساعة العاشرة إلا ربع as-saa-'atul-'aa-shi-rah il-laa rub'	quarter to ten
الساعة العاشرة إلا عشر دقائق as-saa-'atul-'aa-shi-rah il-laa 'ash-ru da-qaa-iq	9:50

What is the date? ما التاريخ؟
mat-taa-riikh?

It's the 16th إنه السادس عشر من سبتمبر/أيلول
September 2007 ٢٠٠٧
in-na-hu as-saa-di-sa 'a-sh-r min
sib-tam-bar/ay-luul 2007

| today | اليوم |
| | al-yawm |

| tomorrow | غدا |
| | qa-dan |

| yesterday | أمس |
| | ams |

Time phrases

. . . .

| When does it begin? | متى يبدأ؟ |
| | ma-taa yab-da? |

| When does it finish? | متى ينتهي؟ |
| | ma-taa yan-ta-hii? |

| When does it open? | متى يفتح؟ |
| | ma-taa yaf-tah? |

| When does it close? | متى يغلق؟ |
| | ma-taa yuq-liq? |

When does it leave?	متى يغادر؟ ma-taa yu-qaa-dir?
When does it return?	متى يعود؟ ma-taa ya-'uud?
at 3 o'clock	في السَّاعة الثَّالثة fis-saa-'a-tith-thaa-li-tha
before 3 o'clock	قبل السَّاعة الثَّالثة qab-la as-saa-'a ath-thaa-li-tha
after 3 o'clock	بعد السَّاعة الثَّالثة ba'-da as-saa-'a ath-thaa-li-tha
in the morning	في الصباح fis-sa-baah
this morning	هذا الصباح haa-thas-sa-baah
in the afternoon (until dusk)	بعد الظهر ba'-dath-thuhr

in the evening (after dusk)	في المساء fil-ma-saa
in an hour's time	خلال مدّة ساعة khi-laa-la saa-'ah

Eating out

Eating places

كشك kushk
Snack bar or street stall that sells sandwiches and pastries

دكان الكباب dukan al kabab
Small kebab shop

مخبز makhbaz
Serves pitta bread with a variety of toppings. Arabic equivalent of a pizzeria

محل الكعك و الحلويات mahal ka'ak wa hul wiyat
Cake shop that serves cakes, pastries and soft drinks

مطعم mat'am

Licensed restaurant with waiter service.
Although lunch is normally served from 12 to
2 pm and dinner from 7 to 10 pm, restaurants
in Turkey will usually serve food outside these
times as well

كافتريا cafteria

Serves a selection of ready-prepared dishes

In a café

. . . .

FACE TO FACE

A ماذا تحبّ؟

maa-thaa tu-hib?

What would you like?

B شاي بالحليب رجاءا

shaay bil ha-liib ra-jaa-an

A tea with milk please

| A ... please | رجاءً ... |
| | ...ra-jaa-an |

| two ... please | ٢ ... رجاءً |
| | 2 ... ra-jaa-an |

| three ... please | ٣ ... رجاءً |
| | 3 ... ra-jaa-an |

| Do you have...? | هل عندك ...؟ |
| | hal 'in-da-ka...? |

| Do you have coffee? | هل عندك قهوة؟ |
| | hal 'in-da-ka qah-wa? |

| Do you have orange juice? | هل عندك عصير برتقال؟ |
| | hal 'in-da-ka as ir bur tu kal? |

| A bottle of sparkling water | قنينة من الماء الفوّار |
| | qin-nii-na min al-maa al-faw-waar |

| sparkling (water) | الماء الفوّار |
| | al-maa al-faw-waar |

| mineral (still water) | ماء معدني (ماء عادي) |
| | maa ma'-da-ni (maa 'aadi) |

A cappuccino, please	كابتشينو، رجاء
	kabat-chii-noo, ra-jaa-an
A tea, please	شاي، رجاء
	shaay, ra-jaa-an
with milk	بالحليب
	bil-ha-liib
with lemon	بالليمون
	bil-lay-muun
with ice	بالثلج
	bith-thalj
with sugar	بالسكّر
	bis-suk-kar
without sugar	بدون سكّر
	bi-duun suk-kar
one more, please	واحد آخر، رجاء
	waa-hid aa-khar, ra-jaa-an

In a restaurant

. . . .

You will never be stuck for somewhere to eat in most Arab countries. There are eating places everywhere, and they are usually open from early in the morning until late at night. If you were planning to eat a full meal, you would begin with مقبلات mu-qab-bilaat (starter), followed by الوجبة الرئيسية al-waj-bah ar-ra-ii-siy-yah (main course), and end with حلوى hal-waa (dessert), or just tea or coffee. Dinner is a very sociable occasion: people often sit and talk for hours.

Food is mostly served warm rather than hot, with the exception of soup.

Is there a good restaurant?	هل هناك مطعم جيد؟ hal hu-naa-ka mat-'am jay-yid?
The menu, please	القائمة، رجاء al-qaa-i-ma, ra-jaa-an
Is there a set menu?	هل هناك قائمة طعام؟ hal hu-naa-ka qaa-i-ma-tu ta-'aam?

148

| What is this? | ما هذا؟ |
| | maa haa-thaa? |

| I'd like this | أنا أريد هذا |
| | anaa u-rii-du haa-thaa |

| What is the speciality of the house? | ما اختصاص المطعم؟ |
| | maa ikh-ti-saa-sul mat'am? |

| with chips | بالبطاطس |
| | bil-ba-taa-tis |

| with salad | بالسلطة |
| | bis-sa-la-da |

| no onion, please | بدون بصل، رجاء |
| | bi-duun ba-sal, ra-jaa-an |

| no tomatoes, please | بدون طماطم، رجاء |
| | bi-duun ta-maa-tim, ra-jaa-an |

| Excuse me! | لو سمحت! |
| | law sa-mah-t! |

| The bill, please | الحساب، لو سمحت |
| | al-hi-saab, law sa-mah-t |

Some more bread, please	مزيدا من الخبز، رجاءً ma-zii-dan minal-khubz, ra-jaa-an
Some more water, please	مزيدا من الماء، رجاءً ma-zii-dan minal al-maa, ra-jaa-an
salt	الملح al-mil-h
pepper	الفلفل al-fil-fil
Another bottle, please	زجاجة اخرى، رجاءً zu-jaa-ja-tun u-kh-raa, ra-jaa-an
Another glass, please	كأس اخر، رجاءً ka-sun aa-khar, ra-jaa-an

Vegetarian

• • • • • • • • • • • • • • • • • • • •

There are no specialist vegetarian restaurants.
In any restaurant, however, there are vegetarian
dishes available.

I am vegetarian	أنا نباتيُ
	anaa na-baa-ti
I don't eat meat	أنا لا آكلُ لحمَ
	anaa laa aa-ku-lul-lahma
Is there meat in this?	هَلْ هناك لحم في هذا؟
	hal hu-naa-ka lahm fii haa-thaa?
What is there without meat?	هل هناك شيء بدون لحم؟
	hal hu-naa-ka she-y bi-duun lahm?

Wines and spirits

Alcohol is forbidden by Islam, although some Arabs drink. In some Arab countries, the possession of alcohol is strictly forbidden to everyone. In other countries, like Iraq, it is legal and available to foreigners.

The wine list, please	قائمة الخمر، رجاءً qaa-i-ma-tul- kham-ri, ra-jaa-an
Can you recommend a good wine?	هلْ بالإمكان أنْ تَنصحني بخمر جيد؟ hal bil-im-kaa-ni an tan-sah-nii bi kham-rin jay-yid?
A bottle of...	زجاجة من... zu-jaa-jah min...
red wine	خمر أحمر kham-r ah-mar

rosé wine	خمر وردي	
	kham-r war-di	
white wine	خمر أبيض	
	kham-r ab-yad	
A glass of...	كأس من...	
	ka-s min...	
a dry wine	خمر جاف	
	kham-r jaaf	
a local wine	خمر محلي	
	kham-r ma-hal-lii	
a sweet wine	خمر حلو	
	kham-r hil-w	
What liqueurs do you have?	أي الخمور عندك؟	
	ay-yul khu-muu-ri 'in-dak?	

Menu reader

Below are some dishes from different countries. Names of dishes are written in the local dialect of each country which might be different from the classical Arabic.

Egypt

....

aish عيش
  bread

asab عصاب
  sugar cane juice

ayesh beladi عيش بلدي
  flat pitta bread made with wholemeal flour

ayesh shami عيش شامي
  flat pitta bread made with white flour

baba ghanoush بابا غنوش
  baked aubergine ground with tahini (paste made from seasme seeds), spices and garlic

baklawa بقلاوة
a baked pastry made of layers of filo dough and nuts
and covered with syrup

bamia بامية
meat and okra stew

basal akhdar بصل أخضر
green onions

basboosa بسبوسة
semolina cake with honey-lemon syrup

bastermah (or **basterma**) بسطرمة
dried cured beef

batarekh بتاركه
salted and dried fish roe

batt baladi بط بلدي
duck

beid hhamine بيض حامين
Egyptian slow-cooked eggs

belah بلح
dates

besara بصارة
mashed broad beans made into a purée and cooked

biram ruzz بيرام رز
baked rice with chicken

couscous كسكس
a dish based on savoury semolina that can be
combined with egg, chicken, lamb or vegetables

esh es seraya عيش السرايا
sweet made with bread and honey

falafel فلافل
blend of broad beans, parsley, garlic and herbs, shaped
into patties and deep-fried

fegl فجل
radish

feteer meshaltet فطير مشلت
Egyptian puff pastry with dips

fireek فريك
toasted wheat

fiteer فطير
round pastry made with layers of filo dough and butter

fool akhdar فول أخضر
fresh green broad beans, eaten with white cheese

fool medames فول مدمس
broad bean stew

fool nabet فول نابت
broad bean soup

fool nabit
sprouted broad beans

gargeer جرجير
watercress

gargir جارجير
Egyptian rocket

gebnah areesh جبنة عريش
white cheese

gibna beida جبنة بيضاء
feta-style cheese

gibna rumy جبنة رومي
cheddar-style cheese

guafa جوافة
guava

hamam mahshi حمام محشي
pigeons stuffed with bulgur wheat

hammem حمام
pigeon

hummus حمص
chickpeas puréed with tahini and lemon and served
as a dip

hummus bi tahini حمص بالطحينة
chickpea and sesame dip

irk sous عرق سوس
liquorice root drink

korrat كرات
leeks

koshari كشري
red lentils and rice

kuftat كفتة
spiced meatballs

kunafa كنافة
baked pastry made of layers of shredded wheat dough
and nuts and covered with syrup

lebb لب
roasted watermelon seeds

lebb abyad لب أبيض
roasted pumpkin seeds

lebb suri لب سوري
roasted sunflower seeds

maashi محشي
stuffed vegetables

mekhalel مخلل
pickles

malana ملانا
green chickpea shoots

meshmesheyya مشمشية
dried apricots

mihallabiya مهلبية
rose-scented pudding

milookhiyya (molokheyya) ملوخية
green herb soup

mish ميش
fermented cheese

mulukhiyyah ملوخية
spinach-like vegetable

oom ali أم علي
warm dessert consisting of a pudding with raisins and
coconut and a cereal topping

qahwa قهوة
coffee

romann رمان
pomegranate

roz bel laban رز باللبن
rice and milk

sardeen memalla سردين مملح
salted sardines

sasal eswed عسل أسود
molasses

seish baladi عيش بلدي
bread made of whole wheat flour

seish dorah عيش درة
bread made from corn flour

seish saymeen عيش صايمين
fasting people's bread

seish shami عيش شامي
pitta bread

sudani سوداني
peanuts

tahini طحينة
sesame seed paste. Often served mildly spiced with
lemon, garlic, salt and pepper as a dip for bread

tammeya تمية
fried vegetable patty made of ground broad beans
(fool) and spices

taratour طرطور
sesame sauce

teen تين
figs

teen shoki تين شوكي
prickly pear

toot توت
mulberry fruit. There are two types, red and white.

torshi ترشي
pickled vegetables.

161

umm ali أم علي
pastry with milk, sugar and raisins

Morocco
. . . .

amalou عمالو
argan oil, almond paste and honey spread

eghrir الغرير
Moroccan pancakes

bistteeya, basteela, or pastilla بستية
puffed pastry stuffed with chicken, eggs and almonds
baked and covered with powdered sugar and
cinnamon

brik bil lahm بريك باللحم
lamb turnover

briouat بريوات
stuffed pastry triangle

briouat bel Kofta بريوات بالكفتة
stuffed pastry triangle with minced meat and spices

chabakiya شبكية
Moroccan sweet

charmoula (chermoula) شرمولة
tangy sauce made from cumin, lemon juice, salt,
black pepper, sweet paprika, ginger, marjoram, and
olive oil

chakchouka شكشوكة
peppers, garlic, cumin and tomatoes cooked with
harissa and olive oil, with eggs

chroba fassia شربة فاسية
vegetable soup, originally from Fez city

couscous كسكسو
a dish based on savoury semolina that can be
combined with egg, chicken, lamb or vegetables

dejaj laimoun دجاج ليمون
chicken with lemons

djej emshmel دجاج مشمل
roasted chicken cooked with olives and lemon

djej bil einab دجاج بالعنب
chicken with grapes

djej Kdra Touimiya دجاج كدرا طعمية
chicken with almonds and chickpeas

djaja mahamara دجاجة محمرة
chicken stuffed with almonds, semolina and raisins

djeja M'Qalli دجاج مقلي
chicken with coriander & mint

feqqas فقاس
biscuits with aniseed and orange blossom

ferakh maamer فراخ معمر
spring chicken with couscous stuffing

ghoriba غريبة
biscuits covered in almonds or sesame seeds

halwa shebakia حلوى شبكية
sesame biscuits eaten during Ramadan

harcha حرشة
semolina pancakes

harira حريرة
vegetable soup with lamb, lentils, tomatoes, chickpeas
and spices. National soup of Morocco, cooked during
Ramadan

harissa هريسة
garlic, chilli, salt and olive oil paste usually served with
couscous

hout حوت
fish stew

kaab-el-ghzal كعب الغزال
('gazelle's horns') pastry stuffed with almond paste
and topped with sugar

kamfounata كمفوناتة
Moroccan ratatouille

kamoun كمون
  cumin

kasbour كزبر
  coriander

kefta كفته
  meatballs

kharkoum كركم
  turmeric

kisra or **khboz** كسرة أو خبز
  leavened bread flavoured with aniseed

khboz bishemar خبز بشمار
  Marrakesh 'pizza'

khubz araby خبر عربي
  pocket bread

kouclas bi khobz ككلاس بالخبز
  bread dumplings

kouclas bi ruz ككلاس بالرز
  rice dumplings

haloua tpolo حلاوة تبولو
  chocolate-sesame cones

hut b'Noua حوت بالنوة
  fish with almond paste

hut bu-Etob حوت بالبلح
  fish stuffed with dates

lahm el Mahammer لحم محمر
lamb in a red sauce

Lahm Maqli لحم مقلي
lamb with olives and lemons

lahm Mashwi لحم مشوي
lamb kebabs

leben لبن
popular milk drink

libzar لبزار
pepper

maadnous معدنوس
parsley

matbucha مطبوشة
pepper and tomato salad

mahancha محنشة
thin pastry filled with almonds

m'semmen مسمن
pancacke served with honey or sugar

mechoui مشوي
roasted lamb

m'hanncha محنشة
(the snake) coiled almond pastry

mourouzia (mzouria) مروزية
sweet lamb dish with raisins, almonds and honey

mslalla مسللى
  marinated olives

qamama كمامة
  lamb tajine with honey and onions

qubdan كبد
  spiced lamb kebabs

ras-el-hanout رأس الحانوت
  classic blend of spices

rayib رايب
  yoghurt with artichoke hearts

righaif رغاف
  pancake with honey and sesame seeds

sfinj سفنج
  doughnuts

skingbir سكنجبير
  ginger

seffa سفة
  couscous sprinkled with almonds, cinnamon and
  sugar

sharbat شربات
  apple milk drink

shabbakia شبكية
  small cakes fried in oil and coated with honey

shlada bi lichine   شلدا باللشين
  orange and walnut salad

smen   سمن
  butter based cooking oil

tagine   طاجن
  lamb or chicken stew cooked in an earthenware pot
  with vegetables, almonds and plums. If made with fish
  it is called **hout**

tagine barrogog bis basela   طجين برقوق بسبسلا
  lamb tajine with prunes

tfaia   تفايا
  lamb tajine with eggs and almonds

warkha   ورقة
  thin pastry sheets

zaafrane beldi   زعفران بلدي
  saffron

zalouk   زلوك
  salad with aubergines

Tunisia
....

brik   بريك
  triangular shaped envelope of crispy pastry containing
  a lightly cooked egg topped with fresh herbs and tuna

boukha بوخة
  fig brandy

brik à l'oeuf بريك بالبيض
  triangular envelope of crispy pastry containing a whole
  egg and a filling

chakchouka شكشوكة
  type of ratatouille with peppers, tomatoes and egg

couscous كسكسي
  Tunisia's national dish, served with vegetables, lamb,
  poultry or fish

chorba' شربة
  thick soup made with tomatoes, onions and pasta

coucha كوشة
  shoulder of lamb cooked with Cayenne pepper and
  turmeric

felfel mahchi فلفل محشي
  peppers stuffed with meat and served with harissa
  sauce

guenaoia قناوية (بامية)
  lamb or beef stew with chillies, okra, sweet peppers
  and coriander

harissa هريسة
  garlic, chilli, salt and olive oil paste usually served with
  couscous

koucha fil kolla كوشة في القلة
fresh lamb sprinkled with rosemary and spices and
baked in a clay pot

koucha bil aallouch كوشة بالعلوش
shoulder of lamb with potato

halim (halalim) حلالم
noodle soup

lalabli لبلابي
garlic and chickpea soup

makroudh مقروض
syrup-soaked honey cake stuffed with dates

mechouia سلاطة مشوية
salad of grilled sweet peppers, tomatoes and onions
mixed with olive oil and lemon, tuna fish and hard-
boiled eggs

mhalbya محلبية
cake made with rice, nuts and geranium water

merguez مرقاز
small spicy sausages

mloukhia (mloukhiya) ملوخية
beef or lamb stew with bay leaves

Ojja عجة
scrambled eggs mixed with tomatoes, pimentos,
peppers and garlic

osben عصبان

type of sausage

salata batata سلاطة بطاطا

hot potato salad with caraway seeds

samsa صمصة

almond and sesame pastries

shorba frik شربة فريك

lamb soup with tomato paste, coriander and parsley,
served with slices of lemon

michwiya سلاطة مشوية

salad made with grilled tomatoes, peppers and onions

tagine طاجين

lamb or chicken stew cooked in an earthenware pot
with vegetables, almonds and plums

torshi طرشي

pickled turnips

thibarine تيبارين

Tunisian date liquor

yo-yo يويو

doughnuts made with orange juice, deep fried then
dipped in honey syrup

Grammar

Arabic grammar is often found to be difficult and complicated. Like most languages, it adheres to grammatical rules. Below are some important features of Arabic grammar.

Article

The article '**al-**' expresses the definite state of a noun of any gender and number.

Grammatical cases

Arabic has three grammatical cases roughly corresponding to: nominative, genitive and accusative, and three numbers: singular, dual and plural.

Normally, nouns take the ending -**u(n)** in the nominative, -**i(n)** in the genitive and -**a(n)** in the accusative. However, with important exceptions, case is not shown in standard orthography, and it is optional whether to articulate a case ending when speaking or reading aloud.

The plural of a noun is formed by a suffix in some cases (**sound plurals**), but frequently, the vowel structure of a word is changed to form the plural (**broken plurals**). There are a number of patterns to how this is done. Some singular nouns take several plurals. The plurals of nouns representing humans usually use sound plurals. Masculine sound plurals take the forms '**-ūn**' in the nominative and '**-īn**' in the genitive and accusative. In the feminine, the ending is '**-āt**' and is limited in its declension to two forms: one for the nominative, and another for both other cases. For example, '**-ātun**' and '**-ātin**' are possible, but not '**-ātan**'. This pattern can also be used for plurals of non-human nouns.

Genders

Arabic has two genders, expressed by pronominal, verbal and adjectival agreement. Agreement with numerals shows a peculiar 'polarity'. The genders are usually referred to as masculine and feminine.

Verbs

As in many other Semitic languages, Arabic verb formation is based on a (usually) triconsonantal root, which is not a word in itself but contains the semantic core. The consonants **k-t-b**, for example, indicate 'write', **q-r-a** indicate 'read', **a-k-l** indicate 'eat', etc. Words are formed by supplying the root with a vowel structure and with affixes.

Personal pronouns

Person	Singular	Plural	Dual
3rd (m) he/they	huwa	hum	humā
3rd (f) she/they	hiya	hunna	hunna
2nd (m) you	anta	antum	antumā
2nd (f) you	anti	antunna	antunna
1st I	ana	nahnu	(n/a)

Attached pronouns

Enclitic forms of the pronoun may be affixed to nouns (representing genitive case, for example, possession) and to verbs (representing accusative, for example, a direct object). Most of them are clearly related to the full personal pronouns. They are identical in form in both cases, except for the first person singular, which is –ī after nouns (genitive) and –nī after verbs (accusative).

Person	Singular	Plural	Dual
3rd (m) him/them	–hu	–hum	–humā
3rd (f) her/them	–hā	–hunna	–hunna
2nd (m) you	–ka	–kum	–kumā
2nd (f) you	–ki	–kunna	–kunna
1st me/us	–(n)ī/–ya	–nā	(n/a)

Grammar

Public holidays

• •

There are two major Islamic religious holidays, called '**Eid al-Fitr**' and '**Eid al-Adhaa**', each lasting two to three days. They are determined by the lunar calendar, so their dates vary from year to year. The first one is the Feast of Ramadan, which marks the end of the holy month of Ramadan. The second is the Feast of Sacrifice; the most important holiday of the year, which marks the end of the Hadj (pilgrimage) of millions of Muslims to the Holylands of Saudi Arabia.

Grammar

Signs and notices

Most signs in airports and stations are bilingual.
Most shops and restaurants in big cities and
tourist-orientated places have English information
boards as well as Arabic ones.

At the station

المحطة	al-ma-had-da	station
المترو	al-mit-ro	metro
خروج	khu-ruuj	exit
البوابة الغربية	al-baw-waa-bah al-qar-biy-yah	west gate
البوابة الشمالية	al-baw-waa-bah ash-sha-maa-li-ya	north gate
مخرج الطوارئ	makh-raj at-ta-waa-ri	emergency exit
التذكرة	at-that-ka-ra	ticket
جواز السفر	ja-waaz as-sa-far	passport

178

كوبونات	ko-boo-naat	voucher/coupon
قسم المبيعات	qism al-ma-bii-'aat	sales section
الخطوط المحلية	al-khu-tuut al-jaw-wiy-yah	local lines
أطفال	at-faal	children
بالغ	baa-liq	adult
درهم	dir-ham	dirham

Inside the station

الرصيف	ar-ra-siif	platform
المصعد	al-mis-'ad	lift
درج	da-raj	stairs
كرسي المعوقين	kur-si al-mu-'aw-wa-qiin	wheelchair
صعود	su-'uud	going up
هبوط	hu-buut	going down

Vending machine/telephone

ماء	maa'	water
شاي عربي	sha-y 'a-ra-bi	Arabic tea
صراف	sar-raaf	money exchange
نفذ	na-fath	out of stock
عاطل	aa-til	out of order
فكة	fak-ka	change
كشك	kush-k	kiosk
هاتف	haa-tif	telephone
دولي	du-wali	international
محلي	ma-hal-li	national
بطاقة	bi-taa-qa	card
ادفع	id-fa	push
اسحب	is-hab	pull

In the bus

مفتوح	maf-tuuh	open
مغلق	muq-laq	close
ممنوع التدخين	mam-nuu' at-tad-khiin	non-smoking
للتدخين	lit-tad-khiin	smoking

مرحاض	mir-haad	toilet
نساء	ni-saa	women
رجال	ri-jaal	men

On the street (places and related words)

. . . .

مصرف / بنك	mis-raf	bank
صيدلية	say-da-liy-yah	pharmacy
فندق	fun-duq	hotel
مطعم	mat-'am	restaurant
مقهى	maq-haa	coffee shop
مغسلة بخارية	maq-sala bu-khaa-riy-yah	dry-cleaner's
السوق المركزي	as-suuq al-mar-ka-zi	supermarket
مركز الشرطة	mar-kaz ash-shurta	police station
غرف متوفرة	qu-raf mu-ta-waf-fira	room available
لا توجد غرف شاغرة	laa tuu-jad quraf shaa-qira	no vacancies
الدكان مفتوح	ad-duk-kaan maftuuh	shop is open

181

الدكان مغلق	ad-duk-kaan muq-laq	shop is closed
الطوارئ	at-ta-waa-ri	emergency

On the street (other road signs)

خطر	kha-tar	danger
توقّف	ta-waq-qaf	stop
اعبر	u'-bur	cross
تحت الإنشاءات	tah-tal inshaa	under construction
ممنوع	mam-nuu'	prohibited
منعطف الى اليمين	mun-'a-taf ilal-ya-miin	right turning
منعطف الى اليسار	mun-'a-taf ilal-ya-saar	left turning
إلى الأمام	ilal-amaam	straight on
طريق المشاة	ta-riiqul-mushaa	pedestrian path
دراجة	dar-raa-jah	bicycle
سيارة	say-yaa-rah	automobile
مشاة	mu-shaa	pedestrians
جسر المشاة	jisrul-mushaa	pedestrian bridge
إشارة مرور	ishaa-rat mu-ruur	traffic signal

Outside the station/taxi stand

موقف	maw-qif	parking
حافلة	haa-fila	bus
سيارة أجرة	say-yaa-rat uj-ra	taxi
سيارة صغيرة	say-yaa-ra sa-qii-ra	small vehicle
سيارة كبيرة	say-yaa-ra ka-bii-ra	large vehicle
السيارات متوفرة	as-say-yaa-raat mu-ta-wa-fi-ra	cars available

At the restaurant/shop

الفطور	al-fu-tuur	breakfast
الغداء	al-qa-daa	lunch
العشاء	al-'a-shaa	dinner
وجبات الطعام التقليدية	wa-ja-baat at-ta-'aam at-taq-lii-diya	traditional meals
وجبات الطعام الغربية	wa-ja-baat at-ta-'aam al-qar-biy-ya	western meals

الضريبة	ad-da-rii-ba	tax
متضمّن للضريبة ورسم الخدمة	mu-ta-dam-min lid-da-rii-ba wa rasm al-khid-ma	tax and service charge included
غير متضمّن للضريبة ورسم الخدمة خاصة	qayr mu-ta-dam-min lid-da-rii-ba wa rasm al-khid-ma	tax and service charge not included
المشروبات	al-mash-ruu-baat	drinks

A

a (n)

English	Arabic	Transliteration
about	حول	hawl
above	فوق	fawqa
to accept	قبل	qabila
accident	حادث	haadith
ache: it aches	وجع يوجع	waja'a: yuuj'
address	عنوان	'in-waan
admission charge	قيمة الدخول	qiimat addukhuul
adult	بالغ	baaliq
aeroplane	طائرة	taa-irah
after	بعد	ba'd
afternoon	العصر	al-'asr
this afternoon	بعد ظهر اليوم	thuhril-yawm
in the afternoon	بعد الظهر	ba'dath-thuhr
tomorrow afternoon	بعد ظهر الغد	ba'da thuhril-qad
again	ثانية	thaaniyatan
age	العمر	al-'umr
agent	الوكيل	al-wakiil
estate agent	وكيل العقارات	wakiil al-'aqa araat / wakiil
travel agent	وكيل السفريات	as-safariyaat
ago:	مضى	mathaa
ahead: straight ahead	للأمام مباشرة / للأمام	lil-amaam: mubaasharatan / lil-amaam
air conditioning	التكييف	at-takyiif
airport	مطار	mataar
alarm	حرس الإنذار	jaras al-inthaar

English	Arabic	Transliteration
alarm clock	الساعة المنبّهة	as-saa'atul munab-bih
alcohol	الكحول	al-kuhuul
without alcohol	بدون كحول	bidoon kuhuul
all	الكل	al-kul
to be allergic to	حساسية من	hasaa-siyah min
all right (ok)	حسناً	hasanan
alone	وحيد	wahiid
always	دائماً	daa-iman
ambulance	سيارة الإسعاف	sayyaarat is'aaf
America	أمريكا	amnikaa
American	الأمريكي	al-amrikii
and	و	wa
angry	غاضب	qaadib
another	آخر	aakhar
another beer	بيرة أخرى	biira ukhraa
answer	جواب	jawaab
there's no answer (phone)	ليس هناك جواب (هاتف)	laysa hunaaka jawaab (haatif)
to answer	أجاب	ajaaba
answering machine	جهاز الإجابة الآلي	ji-haaz al jia ba al aali
ants	النمل	an-naml
any: have you any matches?	أي: هل لديك أي كبريت؟	ayyu: hal ladayka ayyu kibiit?
apartment	شقة	shuqqah
apple	تفاح	tuffaah
apple juice	عصير التفاح	asiir at-tufaa
April	أبريل/نيسان	abriil/niisaan
arm	ذراع	thiraa'
my arm hurts	ذراعي يؤذيني	thiraa'ii yu-thiinii
to arrest	أعتقل	i'taqala
arrivals	القادمون	al-qaadimuun

English	Arabic (script)	Transliteration
to arrive	وصل	wasala
art gallery	المعرض الفني	al-ma'rad al-fanni
artist	فنان	fannaan
ashtray	منفضة السجائر	minfathat as-sajaa-ir
asthma	الربو	ar-rabuu
at	في	fii
to attack	هاجم	haajama
attack	هجوم	hujuum
heart attack	النوبة القلبية	an-nawba al-qalbiyyah
attention	انتباه	intibaah
attractive	جذّاب	jath-thaab
August	أغسطس/آب	aqustus/aab
aunt	عمة	'ammah
Australia	أستراليا	usturaaliyaa
Australian	أسترالي	usturaalii

English	Arabic (script)	Transliteration
automatic car	سيارة أوتوماتيك	sayyaarah otto-matiik
autumn	خريف	kharif
away: please go away!	بعيداً رجاء إبعد عني!	ba'iidan: rajaa-an ib'id 'annii!
B		
baby	الطفل الرضيع	at-tiflur-radii'
baby food	قداء طفل رضيع	qidaa tifl radii'
babysitter	جليسة الأطفال	raa'iyat al afaal
back (of body)	ظهر (من الجسم)	thahr (min al-jism)
backpack	حقيبة الظهر	haqiibat ath-thahr
bad	سيئ	say-yi
bag	حقيبة	haqiiba
baggage	حقيبة	haqiiba
baggage reclaim	استرداد الحقائب	istrdaad al-haqaa-ib

English	Arabic	Transliteration
baker's	خباز	khabaaz
ball	كرة	kurah
bandage	ضماد	dammaad
bank	مصرف	masraf
bar	حانة	haana
barber	حلاق	hallaaq
bargain	صفقة	safqah
no bargaining	لا مساومة	laa musaawamah
basket	سلة	sallaah
bath	حمام	hammaam
bathroom	حمام	hammaam
with bathroom	مع حمام	bil-hammaam
battery (for car)	بطارية (للسيارة)	bat-taa-riya (lis-sayaarah)
the battery is flat	إن البطارية فارغة	innal-battaariya faariqah
bazaar	سوق	suuq
be	يكون	yakuun
beach	شاطئ	shaati
beautiful	جميل	jamiil
bed	سرير	sariir
double bed	سرير مزدوج	sariir muzdawaj
twin beds	أسرة مزدوجة	asirah muzdawajah
bedclothes	غطاء الفراش	qitaaul-firaash
bedroom	غرفة النوم	qurfatun-nawm
double bedroom	غرفة النوم المزدوجة	qurfat an-nawm al-muzdawaj
single bedroom	غرفة النوم الفردية	qurfat an-nawm al-fardiyyah
bee	نحلة	nahlah
beef	لحم البقر	lahmul baqar
before	قبل ذلك	qabla thaalik
before 4 o'clock	قبل الساعة الرابعة	qablas-saa'ah ar-raabi'ah

before dinner	قبل العشاء	qablal-'ashaa	
to begin	بدأ	bada-a	
behind	وراء	waraa	
to believe	يصدّق	usadiq	
belly-dancing	الرقص الشرقي	ar-raqs ash-sharqi	
below	تحت	tahta	
belt	حزام	hizaam	
money belt	حزام المال	hizaamul-maal	
seat belt	حزام الأمان	hizaamul-al aman	
bend	انحناء	inhinaa	
beside	بجانب (بجانب)	bi-jaanib	
(next to)			
best	الأفضل	al-afthal	
better *(than)*	أفضل (من)	afthal (min)	
bicycle	دراجة هوائية	darraajah hawaa'iya	

big	كبير	kabiir	
bigger	الأكبر	akbar	
biggest	الأكبر	al-akbar	
bill	فاتورة	faatuura	
the bill,	الفاتورة رجاءً	al-faatuura,	
please		rajaa-an	
bin *(for rubbish)*	سلة (القمامة)	salla (lil-qumaama)	
bird	طير	tayr	
birthday	عيد الميلاد	iidul-milaad	
happy	!عيد ميلاد سعيدا	iid milaad sa'iid!	
birthday!			
birthday card	بطاقة عيد ميلاد	bitaa-qat 'iid milaad	
biscuits	بسكويت	baskuwayt	
bit: a bit	قطعة قليلة	qit'a: qaliilan	
bite	عضة (حشرة ، كلب)	ad-dah	
(insect, dog)		(hasharah, kalb)	

English		
bitter (taste)	مر (طعم)	mur (ta'aam)
black	أسود	as-wad
blanket	بطانية	bataaniyyah
to bleed	نزف	nazafa
blind (person)	أعمى (على الشخص)	a'maa (shakhs)
blinds (on window)	ستائر (على النافذة)	sataa-ir ('alaan-naaftha)
blister	بثرة	bathrah
blocked	مسدود	masduud
blood	دم	dam
blood group	فصيلة الدم	fasiilatud-dam
blood pressure	ضغط الدم	daqdud-dam
blue	أزرق	azraq
boarding card	بطاقة الركوب	bitaaqat rukuub
boat	مركب	markab
boat trip	رحلة الباخرة	al-baakhirah

English		
boiled (food)	مغلي (غذاء)	maqlii (qithaa)
bone	عظم	athm
book	كتاب	kitaab
to book	حجز	hajaza
booking	حجز	haji
bookshop	مكتبة	maktabah
boots	جزم	jizam
bottle	قنينة	qin-niinah
a bottle of water	قنينة الماء	qinniinatu maa
bottle opener	فتاحة قنينة	fattaahat qinniinah
box	صندوق	sunduuq
box office	شباك التذاكر	shubbaak at-tathaakir
boy	ولد	walad
boyfriend	صديق	sadiiq
brandy	براندي	braandii

English	Arabic	
bread	خبز	khubz
to break	كسر	kasara
to break down (car)	تعطلت (سيارة)	ta'attalat (sayyaarah)
breakfast	فطور	futuur
breakfast included	الفطور و مشمول	alfutuur mashmuul
to breathe	تنفس	tanafasa
bring	احضر	ah-thir
British	بريطاني	britaani
brochure	الدليل	ad-daliil
broken	مكسور	maksuur
broken down (car, machine)	تعطل (سيارة) ماكنة	ta'addala (sayyaarah, maakinah)
brother	أخ	akh
brown	أسمر	asmar
brush	فرشاة	furshaa

English	Arabic	
hairbrush	فرشاة الشعر	furshaatush-sha'r
toothbrush	فرشاة اسنان	furshaatu asnaan
bucket	سطل	satl
bulb (light)	لمبة	lamba
bureau de change	مكتب الصرافة	maktab as-sarraafa
burglary: there's been a burglary	سرقة: هناك سرقة	sirqa: hunaaka sirqa
to burn	احرق	ahraqa
burn	حرقة	hurqah
burnt: it's burnt	احترق هو احترق	ihtaraqa: huwa ihtaraqa
business	تجارة	tijaara
bus station	محطة الحافلات	mahattat al-haafilaat
bus stop	موقف الحافلات	mawqif al-haafilaat

busy: I'm busy	مشغول: أنا مشغول	mashquul: anaa mashquul
butcher's	الجزّار	al-jazzaar
butter	الزبدة	az-zubda
to buy	اشترى	ishtaraa
can I buy this?	هل بالإمكان أن أشترى هذا؟	hal bil imkaani an ashtarii haathaa?
by	بـ	bi
by bus	بالحافلة	bil-haafilaa
by train	بالقطار	bil-qitaar
C		
café	مقهى	maqhaa
cake	كعكة	ka'kah
cake shop	دكان الكعك	dukaan al-ka'k
to call (on phone)	أتصل (على الهاتف)	it-tasala (alaal-haatif)

camcorder	آلة تصوير الفيديو	aalat taswiir alfidyo
		an-naqaala
camel	جمل	jamal
camera	آلة التصوير	aalat taswiir
can	يمكن أن	yumkin an
a can of oil	علبة زيت	ilbat zayt
cancel	إلغاء	ilqaa
candle	شمعة	sham'a
can opener	فتاحة العلب	fat-taahat 'ilba
car	سيارة	sayyaarah
by car	بالسيارة	bis-yaarah
car park	موقف سيارات	mawqif sayyaaraat
car seat (for child)	مقعد سيارة (للأطفال)	maq'ad sayyaarah (lil atfaal)
caravan	قافلة	qafila
card	بطاقة	bitaaqa

English – Arabic

English – Arabic

cards (playing)	kuruut (la'ib)	كروت (لعب)	certificate	shahaada	شهادة
carpet (rug)	sajjaadah (bisaat)	سجّادة (بساط)	chain	silsilah	سلسلة
carry	ihmil	احمل	chair	kursi	كرسي
to cash	sarafa	صرف	champagne	shambanyaa	شمبانيا
cash	naqdan	نقدا	change (coins)	al-baaqii (ʻumlaat ma'daniyah)	الباقي (عملات معدنية)
cash desk	nuqtat ad-dafʻ	نقطة الدفع	keep the change	ihtafith bilbaaqii	احتفظ بالباقي
castle	qal'ah	قلعة	to change (money)	sarafa (nuquud)	صرف (نقود)
cat	qit'ah	قطة	changing room	qurfatut-taqyiir	غرفة التغيير
caution	hathir	حذر	charge (fee)	al-qiima	القيمة (أجر)
cave	kahf	كهف	cheap	rakhiis	رخيص
CD	qurs mudmaj	قرص مدمج	cheers!	hathara	حضر
CD player	mushaqil alqurs almudmaj	مشغل القرص المدمج	cheese	hitaafaat!	هتافات!
cemetery	maqbara	مقبرة	chemist's	jubna!	جبنة
central	markazii	مركزي		savdali	صيدلي
central station	al-mahatta al-markaziyya	المحطة المركزية			
town centre	markaz al-balad	مركز البلد			

English	Arabic	Transliteration
night-duty chemist	الصيدلي الليلي	as-saydali al-layli
cheque	شيك	shiik
cheque book	دفتر الشيكات	daftar ash-shiikaat
traveller's cheques	شيكات المسافرين	shiikaat almusaafiriin
cherry	كرز	karaz
chest (of body)	صدر (من الجسم)	sadr (min al-jism)
chewing gum	علكة	ilkah
chickenpox	جديري الماء	judari al-maa
child	طفل	tifl
chips	رقائق البطاطس	raqaa-iq al-bataatis
chocolate	شوكولاتة	shukulaatah
hot chocolate	شوكولاتة ساخنة	shukulaatah shakhina
chop (meat)	قطعة (لحم)	qit'ah (lahm)

English	Arabic	Transliteration
Christmas	عيد الميلاد	iidul-miilaad
church	كنيسة	kaniisa
cigar	سيجار	sijaar
cigarettes	سجائر	sajaa-ir
a packet of cigarettes	علبة سجائر	ulbat sajaa-ir
cinema	سينما	sinima
circus	سيرك	sirk
city	مدينة	madiinah
city centre	مركز المدينة	markaz al-madiinah
to clean	نظف	nath-thafa
clean	نظيف	nathiif
it's not clean:	هو ليس نظيف	huwa laysa nathiif
climbing: to go climbing	التسلق: الذهاب للتسلق	at-tasalluq: ath-thahaab lit-tasalluq
cloakroom	حجرة المعاطف	hujrat al-ma'aatif

English – Arabic

English	Arabic	Transliteration	English	Arabic	Transliteration
clock	ساعة	saa'ah	iced coffee	قهوة مبردة	qahwa mubarrada
close: is it close by?	قريب: هل هو قريب؟	qariib: hal huwa qariib?	instant coffee	قهوة فورية	qahwa fawriyyah
to close	أغلق	aqlaqa	white coffee	قهوة بحليب	qahwa bi-haliib
when does it close?	متى يغلق؟	mataa yuqliqu?	coin	عملة معدنية	umla ma'daniyyah
closed	مغلق	muqlaq	Coke®	كوك	kook
is it closed?	هل هو مغلق؟	hal huwa muqlaq?	cold: I have a cold	زكمة: عندي زكمة	zakmah: 'indii zakmah
clothes	ملابس	malaabis	cold	برودة	buruudah
coast	ساحل	saahil	I'm cold	أنا أشعر بالبرودة	anaa ash'uru bil-buruuda
coat	معطف	mi'taf	colour	لون	lawn
cocoa	كاكاو	kaakaa-w	comb	مشط	mishtun
cockroach	صرصار	sursaar	to come (arrive)	جاء (وصل)	jaa-a (wasala)
coconut	جوز الهند	jawzul-hind	come in!	أدخل!	udkhul!
coffee	قهوة	qahwa	comfortable	مريح	muriih
black coffee	قهوة سوداء	qahwa sawdaa			

English	Arabic	Transliteration
company (business)	شركة (أعمال)	sharika ('amal)
compass	بوصلة	buusala
complaint	الشكوى	ash-shakwaa
computer	حاسوب	haasuub
concert	حفلة موسيقية	hafla muusiiqiyyah
conditioner (for hair)	مكيّف (للشعر)	mukayyif (lish-sha'r)
condoms	الواقيات الجنسية	al-waaqiyaat al-jinsiyyah
conference	مؤتمر	mu-tamar
to confirm	تأكيد	ta-kiid
congratulations!	مبروك!	mabruuk!
connection (train, plane)	اتصال (قطار، طائرة)	ittisaal (qitaar, taa-irah)
consulate	قنصلية	qunsuliyyah
British consulate	القنصلية البريطانية	al-qunsuliyyah al-britaaniyyah
American consulate	القنصلية الأمريكية	al-qunsuliyyah al-amriikiyyah
contact lens	عدسات لاصقة	adasaat laasiqa
contact lens cleaner	منظف العدسات اللاصقة	munathif al'adasaat al-laasiqa
contraceptives (pill)	موانع الحمل (حبة)	mawaani' al-haml (habbah)
to cook	طبخ	tabakha
cooker	طباخ	tabbaakh
to copy (photocopy)	نسخ (نسخ)	nasakha
copy	نسخة	nuskhah
corkscrew	مفتاح	muftaah
corner	زاوية	zaawiyah
cot	مهد	mahd

English – Arabic

English – Arabic

English	Arabic	Transliteration
cost: how much does it cost?	يكلّف؟ كم يكلّف	yukallif: kam yukallif?
cotton (material)	قطن (مادّة)	qutn (maaddah)
is it cotton?	هل هذا قطن؟	hal haathaa qutn?
to cough	يسعل	yas'al
counter	الضاد	ad-daad
country (not town)	قرية (ليست مدينة)	qaryah (laysat madiinah)
couple (two people)	زوج (شخصان)	zawj (shakhssaan)
crash (collision)	تحطّم	tahaddum
crash helmet	خوذة الأمان	khawthat al-amaan
cream (dairy)	قشطة (معمل الألبان)	qishta (ma'mal albaan)
(cosmetic)	دهن (شكلي)	duhn (shakli)

English	Arabic	Transliteration
credit card	بطاقة الائتمان	bitaaqatul-i-timaan
crisps	رقائق بطاطس	raqaa-iq al-bataatis
crossroads	تقاطع الطرق	taqaaadu' at-turuq
to cry (weep)	بكى (يبكي)	bakaa (yabkii)
cucumber	خيار	khayaar
cul-de-sac	الطريق المسدود	at-tariq masduud
cup	كأس	ka-s
cupboard	دولاب	duulaab
currant	كشمش	kishmish
current	تيار	tayyaar
cushion	وسادة	wisaada
customs	عادات	aadaat
customs control	الرقابة الجمركية	al-jumrukiyya ar-raqaaba
to cut	قطع	qada'a

English	Arabic	
cut	قطعة	qit'a
to cycle	يركب الدراجة الهوائية	yarkab adraja al hawai'ya

D

daily	يوميا	yawmiyyan
damage	ضرر	darar
dance	رقص	raqs
to dance	رقص	raqasa
danger	خطر	khatar
dangerous	خطير	khatir
dark	ظلام	thalaam
date (calendar)	تاريخ (التقويم)	taariikh
date of birth	تاريخ الميلاد	taariikh al-milaad
dates (fruit)	تمر (فاكهة)	tamr (faakiha)
daughter	بنت	bint
dawn	الفجر	al-fajr
day	يوم	yawm
every day	كل يوم	kulla yawm

deaf	أصم	asam
decaffeinated coffee	قهوة خالية من الكافئين	qahwa khaaliya minal kaafiin
December	ديسمبر/كانون الأول	disamber/ kaanuun al-awwal
deck chair	كرسي السطح للمركب	kursiy-yul markab
deep	عميق	amiiq
delay	تأخير	ta-khiir
is there a delay?	هل هناك تأخير؟	hal hunaaka ta-khiir?
delicatessen	دكان لبيع الأطعمة الجاهزة	dukkaan li bay' al-at-'ima al-jaahiza
delicious: this is delicious!	لذيذ: هذا لذيذ!	lathiith: haathaa lathiith!
dentist	طبيب الأسنان	tabiibul-asnaan

English – Arabic

English	Arabic	Transliteration	English	Arabic	Transliteration
dentures	اطقم الأسنان	atqumul-asnaan	I'm on a diet	أنا أتبع حمية	anaa attabi'u himyah
deodorant	مزيل الرائحة	muziel	different	مختلف	mukhtalif
department store	المخزن الكبير	ar-rawaa-ih almakhzan al-kabiir	difficult: it's difficult	صعب: هو صعب	sas'b: huwa sa'b
departures	مغادرة	muqaadarah	dinghy	زورق	zawraq
deposit	إيداع	iidaa'	dining room	غرفة الطعام	qurfat at-ta'aam
dessert	حلوى	halwaa	dinner (evening meal)	عشاء (وجبة طعام) مسائية	ashaa (wajbat ta'aam) masaa-iyyah
detergent	منظف	munathif	direct flight	رحلة مباشرة	rihla mubaashira
diabetic	مريض بالسكر	marrid bis-sukkar	directory (telephone)	دليل (هاتف)	daliil (haatif)
dialling code	رمز الاتصال الهاتفي	ramz al-ittisaal al-haatifi	dirty	قذر	qathir
diamond	ماس	maas	disabled (person)	معوّق (شخص)	mu'awwaq (shakhs)
diarrhoea	إسهال	is-haal	disco	ديسكو	disko
diary	مفكرة	mufakkira	discount	تخفيض	takhfiith
dictionary	قاموس	qaamuus			
diesel	ديزل	dizal			
diet	حمية (رجيم)	himyah (riiim)			

English	Arabic	Transliteration
disease	مرض	marath
disinfectant	مطهر	mutahhir
to dive	غاص	qaasa
divorced	مطلق	mutalliq
I'm divorced	أنا مطلق	anaa mutalliq
dizzy: I feel	دوخة: أحس	dawkha: ahissu
dizzy	بالدوخة	bid-dawkhka
doctor	طبيب	tabiib
documents	وثائق	wathaa-iq
dog	كلب	kalb
doll	دمية	dumyah
donkey	حمار	himaar
door	باب	baab
double bed	سرير مزدوج	sariir muzdawaj
double room	غرفة ذات سريرين	qurfa thaatu sariirayn
downstairs	الطابق السفلي	at-taabiq as-suflii
dozen	دزينة	daziina

English	Arabic	Transliteration
drain	بالوعة	baaluu'a
drawer	درج	daraj
dress	لباس	libaas
to drink	شرب	shariba
drink	شراب	sharaab
drinking water	ماء صالح للشرب	maa saalih lish-shurb
to drive	قاد	qaad
driver	سائق	saa-iq
driving licence	رخصة القيادة	rukhsatul-qiyaada
to drown	غرق	qariqa
drug	مخدر	mukhaddir
drunk	سكران	sakraan
I'm drunk	أنا سكران	anaa sakraan
dry	جاف	jaaf
dry-cleaner's	التنظيف الجاف	attanthiif al-jaaf
dust	غبار	qubaar

English – Arabic

duty-free	غير خاضع للضريبة	qayr khaa-thi' lith-thariiba	e-mail	البريد الإلكتروني	al-bariid al-iliktrony
E			embassy	السفارة	as-safaara
ear	أذن	uthun	*American embassy*	السفارة الأمريكية	as-safaara al-amriikiyyah
early	مبكر	mubakkir	*British embassy*	السفارة البريطانية	as-safaara al-britaaniyyah
earrings	أقراط (حلق الأذن)	aqraat (hilaq al-uthun)	emergency	طوارئ	tawaari
earthquake	زلزال	zilzaal	empty	فارغ	faariq
east	شرق	sharq	end	ان ينتهي	an-nihaa-yah
Easter	عيد الفصح	iid al-fash	*when does it end?*	متى ينتهي؟	mataa yahtahii?
easy	سهل	sahl	engaged (to be married)	خاطب (لكي يتزوج)	khaatib (likay yatazawwaj)
to eat	أكل	akala	*it's engaged* (phone, toilet)	هو مشغول (هاتف، مرحاض)	huwa mashquul (haatif, mirhaath)
egg	بيض	bayd	engine	محرك	muharrik
electric	كهربائي	kahrubaa-ii			
electric razor	شفرة الحلاقة الكهربائية	shafrat al-hilaaqa al-kahrabaa-iyyah			

escape:		
fire escape	سلم النجاة	al-huruub: sullam annajaah
Europe	أوروبا	orobbaa
evening	المساء	al-masaa
this evening	هذا المساء	haathal-masaa
tomorrow evening	مساء غد	masaa-u qad
evening meal	وجبة الطعام المسائية	wajbat-tud-da'aam
every	كل	kullu
every day	كل يوم	kulla yawm
every year	كل سنة	kulla sanah
everyone	كل شخص	kulla shakhs
excellent	ممتاز	mumtaaz
excess luggage	الأمتعة الإضافية	al-amti'a al-ithaafiyyah
exchange	تبادل	tabaadul
exchange rate	سعر الصرف	si'rus-sarf

England	إنكلترا	ingeltraa
English (nationality)	إنكليزي (جنسية)	ingiliiziyyah (jinsiyyah)
(language)	(لغة)	ingliizii
I'm English	أنا إنكليزي	anaa ingliizii
do you speak English?	هل تتكلم الإنكليزية؟	hal tatakallamul-ingliiziyyah?
enjoy: I enjoy swimming	أتمتع بالسباحة	tamatu'u: atamatta'u bissibaaha
enough	كافٍ	kaafin
it's not enough	غير كافٍ	qayr kaafin
enquiry desk	منضدة تحقيق	mindadat tahqiq
to enter	دخل	dakhala
entertainment	ترفيه	tarfih
entrance	مدخل	madkhal
entrance fee	سعر الدخول	si'rud-dukhuul
envelope	ظرف	tharf

English – Arabic

exciting	الإثارة	al-ithaarah
excuse me!	اعذرني!	u'thurnii!
exhibition	معرض	ma'rad
exit	خروج	khuruuj
emergency exit	مخرج الطوارئ	makh-raj at-tawaari
expensive	غالي	qaali
to expire	انتهى	inhaa
to explain	توضيح	tawdiih
please explain	رجاءً وضح	rajaa-an waddih
extra	إضافي	idhaafii
eye	عين	ayn

F

face	الوجه	al-wajh
factory	المصنع	al-masna'
to faint	غاب عن الوعي	qaaba 'anil-wa'y
to fall	سقط	saqata
family	العائلة	al-'aa-ilah

my family	عائلتي	aa-i-latii
famous	مشهور	mash-huur
fan	المشجع	al-mushaj-ji'
far: is it far?	بعيد: هل هو بعيد؟	ba'iid: hal huwa ba'iid?
fare	أجرة (قطار،	ujrah: (qitaar,
(train, bus, etc.)	حافلة، الخ)	haafila, alakh)
farm	المزرعة	al-mazra'a
farmer	المزارع	al-muzaari'
fashion	الأزياء	al-az-yaa
fast	الصوم	as-sawm
fat (person)	سمين (شخص)	samiin (shakhs)
fatty	دسم (غذاء)	dasim (qidaa)
father	سمين	samiin
my father	الأب	al-ab
fault (defect)	أبي	abii
favourite	عيب (عيب)	ayb
	مفضل	mufaddal

English	Arabic	
February	فبراير /شباط	fbraayir/shibaat
feel: I feel sick	أشعر: أشعر بالحاجة إلى الغثيان	ash'uru: ash'uru bil-haajati ilaat-taqayyu
feel well	أنا لا أشعر بصحة جيدة	anaa laa ash'uru bi sahhatin jayyida
I feel tired	أشعر بالتعب	ash'uru bitta'ab
ferry	العبّارة	al-'abbaara
few	بضعة	bid'ah
fiancé(e)	خطيب	khatiib
to fill (up)	ملء	mala-a
fill it up!	إملأه!	im-laa!
film	الفلم	al-film
filter	المرشح	al-murashih
to find	وجد	wajada
fine (to be paid)	غرامة (لكي تدفع)	qaraamah (likay tudfa')
fine (weather)	جميل (طقس)	jamiil (taqs)
finish: when does it finish?	النهاية: متى ينتهي؟	annihaaya: matan-nihaaya?
fire	نار	annaar
fire alarm	جرس الحريق	jarasul-hariiq
fire brigade	الإطفائية	al-itfaa-iyyah
fire exit	خرج من الحادثة	makhraj
fire extinguisher	مطفأة الحريق	mitfa-atul hariiq
fireworks	الألعاب النارية	annajaah al-al'aab annaariyyah
first	أول	awwal
the first train	القطار الأول	al-qitaaril-awwal
the first bus	الحافلة الأولى	al-haafila al-uulaa
first aid	الإسعافات الأولية	al-is'aafaat al-awwaliyah

English – Arabic

English	Arabic	Transliteration
first class	الدرجة الأولى	ad-darajah al-uulaa
first floor	الطابق الأول	attaabiq al-awwal
fish	سمك	samak
to fish	صاد	saada
fisherman	صياد السمك	sayyaadus-samak
fishing rod	سنارة الصيد	sannaaratus-sayd
fit: it doesn't fit me	هو لا يلائمني	mulaa-im: huwa laa yulaa-imunii
fix: can you fix it?	هل بالإمكان أن تصلحه؟	aslaha: hal bil imkaani an tuslihahu?
fizzy	فوار	fawwan
flag	علم	alam
flash (for camera)	وميض (للآلة التصوير)	wamiid (lil-aalat attaswiir)
flask	قارورة	qaaruurah
flat (apartment)	شقة (شقة)	shuqqah

English	Arabic	Transliteration
flat	مستوٍ	mustawi
flavour	نكهة	nak-ha
flea	برغوث	barquuth
flight	رحلة	rihla
flood	فيضان	fayadaan
floor	أرضية	ardiyyah
flour	طحين	dahiin
flower	زهرة	zahra
flu	إنفلونزا	influwanza
fly	ذبابة	thubaaba
to fly	طار	taara
fog	ضباب	dabaab
folder	حافظة	haafitha
to follow	أتبع	ittaba'a
food	غذاء	qada
foot	قدم	qadam
football (game)	كرة قدم (لعبة)	kuratul-qadam (lu'bah)

English		Arabic
for	لـ	li
for me	لي	lii
for sale	للبيع	lil-bay'
forbidden	ممنوع	mamnuu'
forecast (weather)	توقع (الطقس)	tawaqqu' (attaqs)
foreign	أجنبي	ajnabi
foreign currency	العملة الأجنبية	al-'umla al-ajnabiyyah
forest	غابة	qaabah
forever	إلى الأبد	ilal-abad
to forget	نسي	nasaa
fork (for eating)	شوكة (لأكل)	shawkah (lil-akl)
forward(s)	للأمام	lil-amaam
fracture	الكسر	al-kasr
free (unoccupied)	شاغر (غير مشغول)	shaaqir (qayr mashquul)

English		Arabic
(costing nothing)	مجانا (لا يكلف)	majaanan (laa yukallifu shay-an)
freezer	ثلاجة	mujammidah
French	فرنسيون	fransiyyuun
frequent	متكرر	mutakarrir
fresh	طازج	taazaj
fresh fish	سمك طازج	samak taazaj
fresh fruit	فاكهة طازجة	faakiha taazijah
fresh milk	حليب طازج	haliib taazaj
fresh vegetables	خضار طازجة	khudaar taazijah
Friday	جمعة	jum'ah
fridge	ثلاجة	thallaajah
fried (food)	مقلي (غذاء)	maqlii (qithaa)
friend	صادق	sadiq
from	من	min

English – Arabic

English	Arabic	Transliteration
front:	أمام: الباب الأمامي	amaam: al-baab
front door		al-amaamii
frozen	مجمد	mujammad
fruit	فاكهة	faakiha
fruit juice	عصير فاكهة	asir faakiha
fruit salad	سلطة الفواكه	saladatul-faakiha
fuel	وقود	waquud
full	كامل	kaamil
full board	وجبات كاملة	wajabaat kaamila
furniture	أثاث	athaath
further on	أبعد	ab'ad
fuse	مصهر	musahhir
the fuse has blown	انفجر الصهر	infajara al-musahhir
G		
gallery (art)	معرض فني (فن)	ma'rad (fan)
game (sport)	لعبة (رياضة)	lu'bah (riyaadah)
(meat)	الصيد (لحم)	as-sayd (lahm)
garage (private) (selling petrol, etc.)	مرآب (خاص) محطة (بيع بنزين، إلخ)	mir-aab (khaas) mahattah (bay' binziin, alakh)
garden	حديقة	hadiqah
garlic	ثوم	thawm
gas	غاز	qaaz
gate	باب	baab
gents toilet	مرحاض الرجال	mirhaadur-rijaal
genuine	أصلي	aslii
German (nationality)	ألماني (جنسية)	almaani (jinsiyyah)
(language)	ألمانية (لغة)	almaaniyyah (luqah)
Germany	ألمانيا	almaaniyaa
to get	يصبح	yusbihu
to get into	دخل	dakhala
to get on board	ركب	rakiba

English		nazala (haafila)			nathaaraat
to get off (bus, etc)	نزل (حافلة)		glasses (spectacles)	نظارات	
gift	هدية	hadiyyah	to go	ذهب	thahaba
gift shop	دكان الهدايا	dukkaan	to go back	عاد	aada
girl	بنت	bint	to go in	دخل	dakhala
girlfriend	صديقة	sadiqa	to go out	خرج	kharaja
to give (give back)	أعطى (يعيد)	a'taa (yu'iidu)	goat	عنزة	'anzah
give way	أفسح الطريق	ifsah at-tariq	gold	ذهب	thahaba
glass (for drink)	كأس (للشراب)	ka-s (lish-sharaab)	golf	غولف	qolf
glass (substance)	زجاجة (مادة)	zujaajah (maaddah)	golf ball	كرة غولف	kurat qolf
a glass of water	كأس من الماء	ka-s min maa	golf club	نادي الغولف	naadii al-qolf
a glass of wine	كأس من النبيذ	ka-s minan-nabiid	golf course	ملعب الغولف	mal'ab al-qolf
			good	جيد	jayyid
			good day	يوم جيد	yawman jayyidan
			good evening	مساء الخير	masaaul-khayr
			good morning	صباح الخير	sabaahul-khayr
			goodbye	مع السلامة	ma'as-salaama
			goodnight	ليلة سعيدة	laylah sa'iidah

English – Arabic

English – Arabic

grandfather	جد	jadd
grandmother	جدة	jaddah
grapefruit	فاكهة الكريب	faakihat al-kreeb
grapefruit juice	عصير فاكهة الكريب	asiir faakihat al-kreeb
grapes	عنب	'inab
greasy: it's too	دهني: هو دهني	duhnii: huwa
greasy (food)	دهني جدا (الغذا)	duhnii jiddan (qithaa)
green	أخضر	akh-tar
greengrocer's	بقال	baqaal
grey	رمادي	ramaadii
grilled	مشوي	mashwii
grocer's	بقال	baqaal
group (of people)	مجموعة (من الناس)	majmuu'ah (minan-naas)
guarantee	ضمان	damaan
guest	ضيف	dayf

guesthouse	دار الضيافة	daarud-diyaafa
guide/ guidebook	دليل/ دليل	daliil
guided tour	الجولة الموجهة	al-jawla al-muwajaha

H

hair	شعر	sha'r
hair dryer	مجفف الشعر	mujaffifush-sha'r
hairbrush	فرشاة الشعر	furshaarush-sha'r
haircut	حلاقة الشعر	hallaaqush-sha'r
hairdresser	مصفف الشعر	musaffifush-sha'r
half	نصف	nisf
half an hour	نصف ساعة	nisf saa'ah
half board	سكن بنصف وجبة	sakan bi nisf wajbah
half bottle	نصف قنينة	nisf qinninah
ham	لحم الخنزير	laham al-khinziir
hand	يد	yad

English	Arabic		English	Arabic	
hand luggage	أمتعة يدوية	amti'ah yadawiyyah	to hear	سمع	sami'a
handbag	حقيبة يدوية	haqibah yadawiyyah	hearing aid	مساعدة سمع	musaa'idat sam'
handmade	صنع يدوي	sun' yadawii	heart	قلب	qalb
to happen	حدث	hadatha	heart attack	نوبة قلبية	nawbah qalbiyyah
what happened?	ماذا حدث؟	maathaa hadath?	heating	تدفئة	tadfi-ah
happy	سعيد	sa'iid	heavy	ثقيل	thaqiil
harbour	ميناء	miinaa	height	ارتفاع	irtifaa'
hard (tough)	بشدة (قاسي)	bishiddah (qaasii)	hello	مرحبا	marhaban
hat	قبعة	qubba'ah	help!	ساعدني!	saa'idnii!
hazelnut	بندقية	bunduqiyyah	to help	ساعد	saa'ada
he	هو	huwa	herbs	أعشاب	a'shaab
head	رأس	ra-s	here	هنا	hunaa
headache	صداع	sudaa'	high	عالي	aalii
I've got a headache	أنا عندي صداع	anaa 'indii sudaa'	high blood pressure	ضغط دم عالي	daqd dam 'aalii
			high chair	كرسي عالي	kursii 'aalii
			to hire	إستأجر	ista-jara

English	Arabic	Transliteration
to hitch-hike	ارتحل	irtahala
holiday	عطلة	'utla
home	بيت	bayt
honey	عسل	'asal
honeymoon	شهر العسل	shahrul 'asal
horse	حصان	hisaan
hospital	مستشفى	mustashfaa
hot	حار	haar
it's too hot	هو حار جداً	huwa haar jiddan
hotel	فندق	funduq
hour	ساعة	saa'ah
in an hour's time	خلال ساعة	khilaal saa'ah
house	بيت	bayt
how?	كيف؟	kayfa?
how many?	كم عدد؟	kam 'adad?
how much?	كم؟	kam?
how are you?	كيف أنت؟	kayfa anta?

English	Arabic	Transliteration
hungry: I'm hungry	جائع: أنا جائع	jaa-i': anaa jaa-i'
hurry: I'm in a hurry	عجلة: أنا في عجلة	'ajala: anaa fii 'ajala
hurt: it hurts	أذى: إنه يؤذي	athaa: innahu yu-aa-thii
husband	زوج	zawj
my husband	زوجي	zawjii
I	أنا	anaa
ice	ثلج	thalj
ice-cream	بوظة	bootha
iced coffee	قهوة مبردة	qahwa mubarradah
iced tea	شاي مبرد	shaa-y mubarrad
iced water	ماء مبرد	maa mubarrad
identification	تعريف	ta'riif
ill	مريض	mariid

English	Arabic	
immediately	فورا	fawran
important	مهم	muhim
included	متضمن	mutadammin
indigestion	عسر الهضم	asrul-hadm
infection	عدوى	'adwaa
information	معلومات	ma'luumaat
information office	مكتب الاستعلامات	matktabul-isti'laamaat
injured	مصاب	musaab
insect	حشرة	ha-sha-rah
insect bite	عضة حشرة	'addatu-hasharah
insect repellent	طارد الحشرات	taaridul-hasharaat
instant coffee	قهوة فورية	qahwa fawriyyah
insurance	تأمين	ta-miin
interesting	مثير	muthiir
international	دولي	duwalii
interpreter	مترجم	mutarjim
to invite	دعا	da'aa
invoice	فاتورة	faatuura
Ireland	آيرلندا	iirlandaa
Irish	آيرلندي	iirlandii
iron (metal)	حديد (معدن)	hadiid (ma'dan)
(for clothes)	كوى (للملابس)	kawaa (lil-malaabis)
island	جزيرة	jaziirah
it	هو/هي	huwa/hiya
itch: it itches	حكة: يحك	hakka: yahukku
J		
jacket	سترة	sutra
leather jacket	سترة جلدية	sutra jildiyyah
jam (food)	مربى (غذاء)	murabbaa (qithaa)
jammed	مسدود	masduud

English – Arabic

English - Arabic

January	يناير/كانون الثاني	yanaayir/ kaanuun ath-thaanii	July	يوليو/تموز	yuulyuu/tamuuz
jar	جرة	jarrah	jumper	بلوز	bluuz
jeans	جينز	jiinz	junction	تقاطع	taqaatu'
jellyfish	قنديل البحر	qindiilul-bahr	June	يونيو/حزيران	yuunyuu/ huzayraan
jewellery	مجوهرات	mujawharaat	**K**		
Jewish	يهودي	yahuudii	to keep	احتفظ	ihtafitha
I'm Jewish	أنا يهودي	anaa yahuudii	key	مفتاح	miftaah
job	وظيفة	wathiifah	my key, please	مفتاحي، رجاءً	miftaahii, rajaa-an
joke:	نكتة: علمه نكتة	nuktah: haathihii	kind: you're very kind	رحيم: أنت رحيم جداً	rahiim: anta rahiim jiddan
it's a joke		nuktatun	to kiss	قبّل	qabbala
journalist	صحفي	sahafi	kitchen	مطبخ	matbakh
journey	رحلة	rihlah	knee	ركبة	rukbah
jug	دورق	dawraq	knife	سكين	sikkiin
juice	عصير	'asiir	to know	علم	'alima
orange juice	عصير البرتقال	'asiirul-burtuqaal	I know	أنا أعلم	anaa 'alammu
tomato juice	عصير الطماطم	'asiirut-tamaatim	I don't know	أنا لا أعلم	anaa laa 'alammu

L

English	Arabic	Transliteration
label (luggage)	علامة (أمتعة)	'alaamah (amti'ah)
ladies (toilet)	مرحاض السيدات	mihaadus-sayyidaat
lake	بحيرة	buhayra
lamb	حمل	hamal
lamp	مصباح	misbaah
landing	هبوط	hubuut
late	متأخر	muta-akhir
sorry I'm late	آسف لأنا متأخر	aasif anaa mu-ta-akhir
later	لاحقا	laahiqan
launderette	مغسلة	maqsalah
laundry service	خدمة الكي جي	khidmat al-makwaji
lawyer	محامي	muhaamii
leather	جلد	jild
to leave	غادر	qaadara
left	متروك	matruuk
left luggage office	محل إيداع الأمتعة المتروكة	mahal iidaa' al-haqaa-ib al-matruuka
leg	ساق	saaq
lemon	ليمون	laymuun
lemonade	شراب الليمون	sharaabul-laymuun
to lend	أعار	a'aar
to let (allow)	سمح (يسمح له)	samaha (yasmahu lahu)
licence (driving)	رخصة (قيادة سيارة)	ruksa (qiyaadat sayyaarah)
life jacket	سترة النجاة	sutratun-najaat
lifeboat	قارب النجاة	qaaribun-najaat
lifeguard	حارس الإنقاذ	haarisul-inqaad
lift (elevator)	مصعد	mis'ad

English	Arabic	Transliteration
light (illumination)	ضوء (إضاءة)	daw (idaa-a)
(lamp)	نور (مصباح)	nuur (misbaah)
(not heavy)	خفيف (ليس ثقيل)	khafiif (laysa thaqiil)
light bulb	مصباح	misbaah
lighter (cigarette)	قداحة (سيجارة)	qaddaaha (sijaara)
to like	أحب	ahabba
linen	بطانة	bataana
lipstick	أحمر الشفاه	ahmarush-shifaah
to listen to	استمع إلى	istama'a ilaa
litter (rubbish)	فضلات (قمامة)	fadalaat (qumaamah)
little (small)	قليلاً (صغير)	qaliilaan (saqiir)
to live	عاش	'aasha

English	Arabic	Transliteration
to lock	قفل	qafala
lock	قفل	qufl
locker (for luggage)	خزانة (للأمتعة)	khazaanah (lil-amti'a)
long	طويل	tawiil
to look for	يبحث عن	bahatha 'an
lorry	الشاحنة	ash-shaa-hina
lost	مفقود	mafquud
lost property office	مكتب الأشياء المفقودة	maktabul-ash-yaa-al-mafquuda
lot: a lot	كثير	kathiir
lotion	مستحضر	mustah-thir
loud	عالي	'aalii
to love	أحب	ahabba
lovely	رائع	raa-i'
lucky	محظوظ	mah-fuuth
luggage	أمتعة	amti'a
lunch	غداء	qadaa

M					
maid	حارية	jaa-riya	maximum speed	السرعة القصوى	as-sur'a alquswaa
main course (of meal)	وجبة رئيسية (من وجبة الطعام)	wajba ra-iisiyyah (min wajbati-ta'aam)	May	مايو / مايس	maayoo/maayis
			meal	وجبة الطعام	wajbatu-ta'aam
to make	جعل	ja'ala	mean: what does it mean?	المعنى: ماذا يعني هذا؟	al-ma'naa: maathaa ya'nii haathaa?
man	رجل	rajul			
manager	المدير	al-mudiir	meat	لحم	lahm
map	خريطة	khariita	meatball	كرة من اللحم	kurah minal-lahm
marble	رخام	rukhaam			
March	مارس / آذار	maaris/aathaar	medicine	طب	tib
marmalade	مربى البرتقال	murabbal-burtuqaal	to meet	اجتمع	ijtama'a
			meeting	اجتماع	ijtimaa'
married	متزوج	muta-zawwij	to mend	أصلح	aslaha
match (game)	مباراة (لعبة)	mubaaraa (lu'bah)	menu	قائمة	qaa-imah
			the menu, please	القائمة رجاء	al-qaa-imah, rajaa-an
matches (light)	كبريت / عود ثقاب (ضوء)	kibriit/'uud thiqaab (daw)	message	رسالة	risaalah

English – Arabic

English	Arabic	transliteration
meter (taxi)	عدّاد (سيارة أجرة)	mitr (sayaaratu ujra)
metre	متر	mitr
microwave (oven)	مايكرويف (فرن)	mikro-weef (furn)
midday	منتصف النهار	muntasafun-nahaar
middle	منتصف	muntasaf
midnight	منتصف الليل	muntasaful-layl
milk	حليب	haliib
mince (meat)	لحم مفروم (لحم)	lahm mafruum (lahm)
mineral water	الماء المعدني	al-maa al-ma'danii
mints	نعناع	ni'naa'
minute	دقيقة	daqiiq
mirror	مرآة	mir-aah

English	Arabic	transliteration
miss (plane, train, etc.)	تفتّ (طائرة، الخ)	taqayyaba (tayyaarah, qitaar)
missing (thing)	فقدان (شيء)	fuqdaan (shay)
mistake	خطأ	khata
monastery	دير	dir
Monday	الإثنين	al-ithnayn
money	مال	maal
month	شهر	shahr
monument	تمثال	timthaal
moon	قمر	qamar
more	أكثر	akthar
some more...	...أكثر	akthar...
morning	صباح	sabaah
in the morning	في الصباح	fis-sabaah
tomorrow morning	صباح الغد	sabaahul-qad
this morning	هذا الصباح	hathaas-sabaah

English			English		
mosque	مسجد	masjid	museum	متحف	mithaf
mosquito net	ناموسية	naamuusiyyah	music shop	دكان موسيقى	dukkaan muusiqaa
mosquitoes	بعوض	ba'uutha	Muslim	مسلم	muslim
mother	أم	al-um	mussels	بلح البحر	balahul-bahr
mother-in-law	عمة	'ammah	mustard	خردل	khardal
motorbike	دراجة نارية	darraajah naariyyah	**N**		
motorway	الطريق السريع	at-tariq as-sarii'	nail (metal)	مسمار (معدن)	mismaar (ma'dan)
mountain	جبل	jabal	(finger, toe)	ظفر (اصبع اصبع)	thifr
mouse	فأر	fa-r	name	الاسم	al-ism
moustache	شارب	shaarib	my name is...	اسمي...	ismii...
mouth	فم	fam	napkin	المنديل	al-mindiil
much	كثير	kathiir	nappy	الحفاظة	al-haafitha
how much?	كم؟	kam?	narrow	ضيق	dayyiq
too much	كثيراً	kathiiran	nationality	الجنسية	al-jinsiyyah
it's too much	هذا أكثر من المقبول	hathaa akthar min ma'quul			
(too expensive)	(غالٍ جداً)	(qaali jiddan)			

English – Arabic

English	Arabic	Transliteration
navy blue	الأزرق الداكن	al-azraq ad-daakin
near	قريب	qariib
necessary	ضروري	tharuurii
neck	الرقبة	ar-raqaba
to need	احتاج	ihtaaja
I need...	...أحتاج	ahtaaju...
I need a car	أحتاج سيارة	ahtaaju sayyaarah
I need to go	أحتاج للذهاب	ahtaaju lith-thahaab
needle	إبرة	al-ibrah
a needle and thread	إبرة وخيط	ibrah wa khayt
neighbour	الجار	al-jaar
nephew	ابن الأخ	ibnul-akh
never	أبدا	abadan
new	جديد	jadiid
news	الأخبار	al-akhbaar
newspaper	الصحيفة	as-sahiifa
an English newspaper	صحيفة إنجليزية	ingliiziyyah
newsstand	كشك بيع الصحف	kushk bay' as-suhuf
New Year	السنة الجديدة	as-sanah al-jadiidah
New Zealand	نيوزيلندا	niyuu zilanda
next	التالي	at-taalii
next to	بجانب	bi-jaanib
nice	لطيف	latiif
it's very nice	هو لطيف جدا	huwa latiif jiddan
niece	ابنة الأخت	ibnatul-ukht
night	الليل	al-layl
last night	ليلة أمس	laylata ams
nightclub	النادي الليلي	annaadii al-ahlii
no	لا	laa

English	Arabic	Transliteration
no, thanks	لا شكراً	laa, shukram
noisy	صاخب	saakhib
non-alcoholic	لا كحولي	laa kuhuulii
a non-alcoholic drink	شراب لا كحولي	sharaab laa kuhuulii
none	لا شيء	laa shay
there's none left	لم يتبقى شيء	lam yatabaqqa shay
non-smoking	لغير المدخنين	li-ghayr al-mudakhiniin
north	الشمال	ash-shamaal
Northern Ireland	آيرلندا الشمالية	iirlanda ash-shamaaliyyah
nose	الأنف	al-anf
not	ليس	laysa
notebook	دفتر الملاحظات	daftar al-mulaahathaat

English	Arabic	Transliteration
nothing	لا شيء	laa shay
November	نوفمبر/تشرين الثاني	nofambar/tishriin ath-thaanii
now	الآن	al-aan
number	العدد	al-'adad
phone number	رقم الهاتف	raqam al-haatif
number plate	رقم السيارة	raqamus-sayyaarah
nurse	الممرضة	al-mumarrithah
nuts (bar nibbles)	بندق (حبة تقضم)	bunduq

O

English	Arabic	Transliteration
October	أكتوبر/تشرين الأول	oktobar/tishriin al-awwal
octopus	أخطبوط	ukhtubuut
off (radio, engine, etc.)	مطفئ (راديو، محرك إلخ)	muntafi (raadyo, muharrik)

English	Arabic	Transliteration	English	Arabic	Transliteration
the heating is off	إن التدفئة منطفئة	innat-tadfi-ata muntafiyah	onion	بصل	basal
office	مكتب	maktab	only: only one	فقط: واحد فقط	faqad: waahid
often	في أغلب الأحيان	fii aqlabil-ahyaan			faqad
oil	نفط	nift	open	مفتوح	maftuuh
OK	حسنا	hasanan	*is it open?*	هل هو مفتوح؟	hal huwa maftuuh?
old (person)	كبير (السن)	kabiirus-sin	to open	فتح	fataha
(thing)	قديم (شيء)	qadiim	opening hours	أوقات الفتح	awqaatul-fath
how old are you?	كم عمرك؟	kam 'umruka?	operator	موظف الاتصالات	mu-wath-thaf
I'm ... years old	أنا ... سنوات	anaa ...	(telephone)	(هاتف)	it-tisaalaat
		sanawaat			(haatif)
olive oil	زيت الزيتون	zaytuz-zaytuun	opposite	نظير	nathiir
olives	زيتون	zaytuun	optician's	فاحص البصر	faahisul-basar
on	على	'alaa	or	أو	aw
once: at once	حالا	haalan	orange (colour)	برتقالي (لون)	burtuqaalii (lawn)
one	واحد	waahid	orange	برتقال	burtuqaal
			orange juice	عصير البرتقال	'asiirul-burtuqaal
			orchestra	أوركسترا	orkestra

English	Arabic	Transliteration
to order (food)	طلب (الغذاء)	talab (qithaa)
other	آخر	aakhar
our	لنا	naa
out	خارج	khaarij
out: out of order	معطل	mu'attal
oven	فرن	furn
to overtake	إجتاز	ijtaaza
to owe	يدين	yudinu
owner	مالك	maalik
P		
to pack (bags)	حزم (حقائب)	hazama (haqaa-ib)
package tour	رحلة منظمة	rihla munath-thama
packet	حزمة	hizmah
painful: it's very painful	مؤلم: هو مؤلم جداً	mu-lim: huwa mu-lim jiddan
painkiller	مضاد الألم	mu-daadul-aalaam
painting (picture)	صورة (صورة)	suurah
pair	زوج	zawj
palace	قصر	qasr
pancake	فطيرة	fatiirah
pants (trousers)	ملابس داخلية (بنطلون)	malaabis daakhiliyyah
paper	ورقة	waraqah
parcel	حزمة	hizmah
parcels counter	مكتب الحزم	marktab al-hizam
pardon!	عفواً!	'afwan!
parents	أباء	aabaa
park	متنزه	muntazah
to park	أوقف	awqafa
part (spare)	قطعة (إحتياطي)	qit'ah (ihtiyaadii)

partner (business)	شريك (عمل)	shariik ('amal)
my partner (in couple)	شريكي (في الزواج)	shariikii (fiz-zawaaj)
party (celebration)	حفلة (احتفال)	haflah (ihtifaal)
passenger	مسافر	musaafir
passport	جواز السفر	jawaazus-safar
passport control	جوازات	jawaazaat
pasta	باستا	baastaa
pastry (cake)	معجنات (كعكة)	mu'ajjanaat (ka'kah)
to pay	دفع	dafa'a
peanuts	فستق	fustuq
pearl	لؤلؤة	lu-lu-ah
pedestrian	ماشي	maashii
pedestrian crossing	منطقة عبور المشاة	mantiqat 'ubuur mushaah
pen	قلم	qalam
pencil	قلم الرصاص	qalamur-rasaas
penicillin	بنسلين	binsiliin
pensioner	متقاعد	mutaqaa'id
pepper (spice)	فلفل (تابل)	filfil (taabil)
pepper (vegetables)	فلفل (خضار)	filfil (khuthaar)
per	بالـ	li-kulli
per hour	بالساعة	bis-saa'ah
per kilometre	لكل كيلومتر	li-kulli kilomitar
per week	بالأسبوع	bil-usbuu'
perfect:		
it's perfect	هذا هو ماثل	mithaalii huwa mithaalii
performance	أداء	adaa
perfume	العطر	al-'itr
person	شخص	shakhs

English	Arabic	Transliteration
pill	حبة	habbah
pillow	وسادة	wisaadah
pin	دبوس	dabbuus
pink	وردي	wardii
pipe (for smoking)	أنبوب (للتدخين)	unbuub (lit-tadkhiin)
(drain, etc.)	أنبوبة (بالوعة)	unbuubah (baaluu'ah)
plain	واضح	waadih
plane	طائرة	taa-irah
plaster	لصقة	lasqah
plastic	بلاستيك	balaastiik
plate	صحن	saahn
platform (railway)	رصيف (سكة حديد)	rasiif (sikkat hadiid)
to play	لعب	lu'bah
please	رجاء	rajaa-an

English	Arabic	Transliteration
per person	الشخص الواحد	lish-shakhs al-waahid
petrol	بنزين	binzin
unleaded petrol	البنزين الخالي من الرصاص	al-binzin al-khaalii minar-rasaas
petrol station	محطة البنزين	mahat-tat al-binzin
phone	هاتف	haatif
phonecard	بطاقة هاتف	bitaaqat haatif
photocopy	استنساخ	insakh
photograph	صورة	suurah
picnic	نزهة	nuzha
picture (on wall)	صورة (على الحائط)	suurah ('alal haa-it)
pie	فطيرة	fatiirah
piece (slice)	قطعة (شريحة)	qit'ah (shariiha)
pier	رصيف	rasif

English	Arabic	Transliteration
plug (electric)	(مقبك كهربائي)	manfath (kahrubaa-ii)
(for sink)	سدادة (المغسلة)	saddaadah (lil-maqsalah)
plumber	سباك	sabbaak
pocket	جيب	jayb
poisonous	سام	saam
police	شرطة	shurtah
police station	مركز الشرطة	markaz ash-shurtah
polish (for shoes)	صقل (الأحذية)	saql (lil-ah-thiyah)
pool	مسبح	masbah
poor (not rich)	فقير (ليس غني)	faqiir (laysa qani)
pork	لحم الخنزير	lahmul-khinziir
port (harbour)	ميناء (مرسى)	miinaa
porter (for door)	بواب (الباب)	baw-waab

English	Arabic	Transliteration
(for luggage)	حمال (الأمتعة)	habbaal (lil-amti'ah)
possible	محتمل	muhtamal
to post	أرسل	arsala
post office	مكتب البريد	maktabul-bariid
postbox	صندوق البريد	sunduuqul-bariid
postcard	بطاقة بريدية	bitaa-qah bariidiyyah
postcode	رمز بريدي	ramz bariidii
poster	ملصق	mulsaq
pot (for cooking)	قدر (الطبخ)	qidr (lit-tabkh)
potato	بطاطا	bataataa
boiled	بطاطا مغلية	bataataa maqliyyah
potatoes	بطاطا	bataataa
fried potatoes	بطاطا مقلية	maqliyyah
mashed potato	بطاطا مهروسة	bataataa mahruusah

English	Arabic	
potato salad	سلطة بطاطا	salatat bataataa
powdered milk	حليب جاف	haliib jaaf
prawns	جمبري	jambari
prayers	صلاوات	salaawaat
to prefer	فضل	faddala
I'd prefer tea	انا أفضل شاي	anaa ufaddilu shaay
pregnant	حامل	haamil
I'm pregnant	انا حامل	anaa haamilah
prescription	وصفة	wasfah
present (gift)	هدية (هدية)	hadiyyah
this is a present	هذه هدية	haathihii hadiyyah
pretty	جميل	jamil
price	سعر	sir
price list	قائمة الأسعار	qaa-imatul as aar
private	خاص	khaas

English	Arabic	
private bathroom	حمام خاص	hammaam khaas
probably	محتمل	muhtamal
to pronounce	نطق	nataqa
public holiday	عطلة وطنية	'utla wataniyyah
pudding	حلوى	halwaa
to pull	سحب	sahaba
purple	أرجواني	urguwaanii
to push	دفع	dafa'a
pushchair	كرسي مدفوع بعجلة	kursii madfuu'
pyjamas	بيجامة	bijaamah

Q

English	Arabic	
quality	جودة	juudah
good quality	جودة عالية	juudah 'aaliyah
poor quality	جودة رديئة	juudah radii-ah
quay	رصيف الميناء	rasiif al-minaa
queen	ملكة	malikah
question	سؤال	su-aal

to queue	احتفظ	istaffa
queue	طابور	taabuur
quickly	بسرعة	bi-sur'ah
quiet	هدوء	huduu
quilt	لحاف	lihaaf
R		
rabies	داء الكلب	daa-ul-kalb
race (sport)	ركض (رياضة)	rakatha (riyaathah)
radio	راديو	raadyoo
radish	فجل	fijl
railway	سكة الحديد	sikkat hadiid
railway station	عمقة سكة الحديد	sikkatul-hadiid
rain	مطر	matar
raincoat	معطف مطر	mi'taf matar
raisins	زبيب	zabiib
rare (steak)	غير مستوى (ستيك)	qayr mustawii

rash (skin)	طفح (جلد)	dafh (jild)
rat	جرذ	jarath
rate: exchange rate	سعر الصرف	si'r: si'rus-sarf
raw	خام	khaam
razor	شفرة	shafrat
to read (book, etc.)	شفرة الحلاقة	al-hilaaqah
	قرأ (كتاب الخ)	qara-a (kitaab)
ready	جاهز	jaahiz
real	حقيقي/أصلي	haqiiqii/aslii
receipt	إيصال	iisaal
reception (desk)	مكتب الاستقبال	maktabul-istiqbaal
recipe	وصفة	was-fah
to recommend	أوصى	awsaa
red	أحمر	ahmar
red wine	نبيذ أحمر	nabid ahmar

English		
reduction	تخفيض	takhfid
to refund	نقرد مسترجعه	nuquud mustarja'ah
regulations	تعليمات	ta'liimaat
relation (family member)	علاقة (فرد من العائلة)	'ilaaqah (fard min 'aa-ilah)
reliable (person, service)	موثوق (شخص، خدمة)	mawthuuq (shakhs, khidmah)
to remember	تذكر	tathakkara
to rent	إيجار	ista-jara
rent	إيجار	ijjaar
to repair	أصلح	aslaha
to repeat	كرر	karrara
reservation (room, table, etc.)	حجز	haiz
to reserve	حجز (غرفة، المائدة)	hajaza (qurfah, mindatha)
reserved	محجوز	man-juuz
to rest	ارتاح	irtaaha
restaurant	مطعم	mat'am
retired	متقاعد	mutaqaa-'d
to return (ticket)	عاد	'aada
return (ticket)	ذهاب وإياب (تذكرة)	thahaab wa iyaab
reverse-charge call	مكالمة بالدفع المكسي	mukaalamah bid-daf'-aksii
rice (cooked)	رز (مطبوخ)	ruz (matbuukh)
rice (uncooked)	رز (غير مطبوخ)	ruz (qayr matbuukh)
rich (person)	غني (شخص)	qani (shakhs)
rich (food)	غني (قثاء)	qani (qithaa)
right (correct)	صحيح	sahiih
right (not left)	ليس يسار	laysaa yasaar
on/to the right	على / إلى اليمين	'alaa/ilaa al-yamiin

English – Arabic

English	Arabic	Transliteration
ring (for finger)	خاتم (لل‍إصبع)	khaatim (lil-isba')
river	نهر	nahr
road	طريق	tariiq
road map	خارطة	khaaritah
roof	سقف	saqf
room	غرفة	qurfah
room service	خدمة غرفة	khdmat al-qurfah
rope	حبل	habl
rose	وردة	wardah
rotten (food)	متعفن (طعام)	muta affin (qithaa)
route	طريق	tariiq
rowing boat	زورق التجديف	zawraqut-tajthiif
rubber	مطاط	mattaat
rubbish	قمامة	qumaamah
rucksack	الجربندية / حقيبة الظهر	al-jarbindiyyah/ haqiibatuth-thahr
rug	بساط	bisaat

English	Arabic	Transliteration
S		
sad	حزين	haziin
safe (for valuables)	خزنة	khaznah
safe (medicine, etc.)	سلامة (طب)	salaamah (tib)
sailing	الإبحار	al-ibhaar
sale	بيع	bay'
for sale	للبيع	lil-bay'
salad	سلطة	salatah
salesman	بائع	bir-i'
salmon	سلمون	salamuun
salt	ملح	milh
same	نفسه	nafsuhu
sand	رمل	raml
sandals	صنادل	sanaadil
sanitary towel	المنشفة الصحية	alminshafa as-sihwah

English		
sardines	sirdin	سردين
Saturday	sabt	سبت
sauce	salsah	صلصة
saucepan	qidr	قدر
sausage	sajq	سجق
savoury	at-ta'aam almushahii	الطعام الشهي
to say	qaala	قال
school	nmadrasah	مدرسة
scissors	miqas	مقص
scorpion	'aqrab	عقرب
Scotland	iskotlandaa	اسكتلندا
Scottish	iskotlandii	إسكتلندي
sculpture	naht	نحت
sea	bahr	بحر
seafood	al-ma-kuulaat al-bahriyyah	المأكولات البحرية

English		
seat (chair; on bus, train, etc.)	miq'ad (kursi)	مقعد (كرسي)؛ (على قطار، إلخ)
reserved seat	miq'ad mahjuuz	مقعد محجوز
seat belt	hizaamul-miq'ad	حزام المقعد
second	ath-thaaniyah	الثانية
second-class	ad-darajah ath-thaaniyah	الدرجة الثانية
a second-class ticket	that-kara minad-darajah ath-thaaniyah	تذكرة من الدرجة الثانية
second-hand	musta'mal	مستعمل
to see	ra-aa	رأى
to sell	baa'a	باع
to send	arsala	أرسل
senior citizen	musin	مسن
separate	munfasil	منفصل
separately	munfasilan	منفصلاً
September	sibtamber/ayluul	سبتمبر/أيلول

English – Arabic

English		Arabic
serious	حانّي	jiddii
service	خدمة	khidmah
service charge	رسم الخدمة	rasmul-khidmah
set menu	قائمة طعام ثابتة	qaa-imah
		murakkabah
shade (shadow)	ظلّ (ظلال)	thalla (thil)
shallow (water)	ضحل (ماء)	dahl (maa)
shampoo	شامبو	shaamboo
to shave	حلق	halaqa
shaver	آلة الحلاقة	aalatul-halq
shaver socket	مقبس آلة الحلاقة	miqbasu
		aalatil-halq
shaving cream	دهن الحلاقة	duhnil-hilaawah
she	هي	hiya
sheep	خراف	khiraaf
sheet (for bed)	غطاء (السرير)	qitaa (lis-sariir)
shelf	الرفّ	ar-raf
shell	صدفة	sadafah

English		Arabic
shellfish	الأسماك الصدفيّة	al-asmaakus-sadafiyyah
ship	سفينة	safiinah
shirt	قميص	qamiis
shoes	أحذية	ah-thiyah
shop	دكّان	dukaan
shop assistant	عامل دكّان	'aamilud-dukaan
shopping	تسوّق	tasawwuq
short	قصير	qasiir
shorts	شورت (بنطلون قصير)	shoort (bantaloon qasiir)
(short trousers)		
show	معرض	ma'rad
to show	عرض	'arada
shower (bath)	دش (حمّام)	dush (hammaam)
shrimps	روبيان	ruubiyaan
to shut	أغلق	aqlaqa
shut	مغلق	muqlaq

English		Arabic
sick: I feel sick	مريض: أشعر باخدا ابن النحي	mariid: ash'uru bil-haajati ilat-taqayyu
sightseeing	مشاهدة معالم البلدة	mushaahadat ma'aalim al-madinah
sign (road-, notice, etc.)	لافتة (طريق) ملاحظة (الخ)	laaftah (tariiq, mulaahathah)
to sign (form, cheque, etc.)	وقع (الاستمارة (الخ) صناك (الخ)	waqqa'a (istimaarah, shiik)
signature	توقيع	tawqii'
silk	حرير	hariir
is it silk?	هل هو حرير؟	hal huwa hariir?
silver	فضة	fiddah
is it silver?	هل هي فضة؟	hal hiya fiddah?
simple (easy); (unadorned)	بسيط (سهل) (غير مزين)	basiit (sahl) (qayr muzayyan)

English		Arabic
single (tone); (ticket); (unmarried)	وحيد	wahiid
I'm single	أنا وحيد	anaa wahiid
single room	غرفة ذات سرير واحد	qurfah thaatu sariir waahid.
sink	مغسلة	maqsalah
sister	أخت	ukht
sit	اجلس	ijlis
size (shoes)	حجم (الحذية)	hajm (ahthiyah)
bigger size	حجم أكبر	hajm akbar
smaller size	حجم أصغر	hajm asqar
skimmed milk	الحليب القشوط	al-haliib al-muqashat
skin	جلد	jild
skirt	تنورة	tannuurah
sky	سماء	samaa
to sleep	نام	naama

English	Arabic	Transliteration
sleeping bag	كيس النوم	kiisu-nawm
sleeping pill	القرص المنوّم	al-qurs al-munawwim
slice	شريحة	sharihah
slippers	نعال	na'aal
slow	بطيء	batii
small	صغير	saqir
smaller	أصغر	asqar
to smell	شمّ	shamma
smell	رائحة	raa-ihah
smile	إبتسامة	ibtisaamah
to smoke	دخّن	dakh-khana
smoke	دخان	dukh-khaan
I don't smoke	أنا لا أدخّن	anaa laa udakh-khin
snake	أفعى	af'aa
snorkelling	غوص	qaws
soap	صابون	saabuun

English	Arabic	Transliteration
socks	جوارب	jawaarib
socket (electrical)	مقبس (كهرباني)	maqbas (kahrubaa-ii)
soft	ناعم	naa'im
soft drink	مشروب لا كحولي	mashruub laa kuhuulii
sold out	انتهى	intahaa
some	بعض	ba'd
someone	شخص ما	shakhsun maa
something	شيء	shay
sometimes	أحياناً	ahyaanan
son	ابن	ayna
song	أغنية	uqniyah
soon	قريباً	qariiban
sorry: I'm sorry!	آسف! أنا آسف!	aasif! anaa aasif!
sort (type)	نوع (النوع)	naw'
soup	شوربة	shoorbah

English	Arabic		English	Arabic	
south	جنوب	janaub	sponge (for cleaning)	إسفنج (للتنظيف)	isfanj (lit-tanthiif)
souvenir	تحفة	tuhfah	spoon	ملعقة	mil'aqah
souvenir shop	دكان التحف	dukaan attuhaf	sport	رياضة	riyaadah
sparkling	تألق	ta-alluq	spring (season)	ربيع (فصل)	rabii' (fasl)
to speak	تكلّم	takallama	square (in town)	فناء (في البلدة)	fanaa (fil-baldah)
do you speak English?	هل تتكلم الإنجليزية؟	hal tatakallamul-ingliiziyyah?	squid	سمك الصبّار	samakus-sabbaar
I don't speak Arabic	أنا لا أتكلم اللغة العربية	anaa laa atkallamul-luqatal 'arabiyyah	stadium	ملعب	mal'ab
			stairs	سلّم	sullam
			stamp	طابع	taabi'
			star	نجم	najm
special	خاص	khaas	to start	بدأ	bada-a
speed	سرعة	sur'ah	station	محطة	mahattah
spice	تابل	taabil	bus station	محطة الحافلات	mahattatul-haaflaat
spicy	كثير التوابل (حار)	kathiir at-tawaabil (haar)	train station	محطة القطار	mahattatul-qitaar
spirits	أرواح	arwaah	to stay	أقام	aqaama

still (not fizzy)	ساكن (ليس فوار)	saakin (laysa fawwaar)	
to sting	لدغ (عضة)	ladaqa ('adda)	
(bite); (bum)			
wasp sting	لدغة زنبور	ladqat zanbuur	
stomach	معدة	ma'idah	
stop!	قف!	qif!	
storm	عاصفة	aasifah	
straight on	استمر إلى الأمام	istamir ilal-amaam	
keep			
straight on	استمر إلى الأمام	istamir ilal-amaam	
street; major	شارع؛ طريق رئيسي	shaari'; tariiq ra-iisii	
thoroughfare			
street map	خريطة الشوارع	khariidat ash-shawaari'	
string	خيط	khayt	
strong	قوي (شاي؛ قهوة)	qawi (shaay, qahwah)	
(tea, coffee)			

stuck:		iltasaqa: huwa	التصق: هو ملتصق
it's stuck		multasiq	
student	طالب	taalib	
stung: I've	لسعني أنا لسعت	lasa'a: anaa	
been stung		lusi'tu	
stupid	غبي	qabi	
suede	جلد مدبوغ	jild madbuuq	
sugar	سكّر	sukkar	
suit (clothes)	بذلة (ملابس)	badlah (malaabis)	
suitcase	حقيبة	haqiibah	
I've lost my	فقدت حقيبتي	faqat-tu haqibatii	
suitcase			
summer	صيف	sayf	
in summer	في الصيف	fis-sayf	
sun	شمس	shams	
sunbathe	تشمس	tashammus	
sunburn	حرقة الشمس	hurqatush-shams	
Sunday	الأحد	al-ahad	

sunglasses	نظارات شمسية	nath-thaaraat shamsiyyah
sunshade	ظلة / مظلة	shamsiyyah/ mithallah
sunstroke	ضربة الشمس	darbatush-shams
suntan lotion	مستحضر السمرة	mustah-thar as-sumrah
supermarket	السوق المركزي	assuq al-markazii
supplement	ملحق	mulhaq
surfboard	لوح التزلج	lawh attazalluj
surfing	تزلج	tazaluj
surname	اللقب	allaqab
sweater	بلوز	bluuz
sweet	حلوى	halwaa
sweetener	محلي	muhallii
sweets	حلويات	halawiyyaat
to swim	سبح	sabaha

swimming pool	مسبح	masbah
is there a swimming pool?	هل هناك مسبح؟	hal hunaaka masbah?
swimsuit	كسوة السباحة	kiswat as-sibaaha
switch	مفتاح	miftaah
to switch on	شغل	shaqqala
to switch off	أطفأ	atfa-a
swollen (finger, ankle, etc)	انتفخه (إصبع، كاحل إلخ)	intafakha (isba', kaahil)

T

table	طاولة	taawilah
table tennis	كرة الطاولة	kuratud-daawilah
to take	أخذ	akhatha
can I take pictures?	هل مسموح أن أصور؟	hal masmuuh an usawwir?

English – Arabic

English	Arabic	Transliteration
will you take a picture of us?	ممكن تلتقط صورة لنا؟	mumkin taltaqid suurah minnaa?
to talk	نكلم	takallama
tall	طويل	tawiil
tap	صنبور	sunbuur
tape (cassette)	شريط (كاسيت)	sharit (kaseet)
taste: can I taste some?	ذوق هل بالإمكان أن أتذوق منه؟	thawq: hal bil-imkaani an atathawwaqa haathaa?
tasty	لذيذ	lathiith
tax	ضريبة	thariibah
taxi	سيارة الأجرة	sayyaaratul-ujrah
tea	شاي	shaay
teabag	كيس الشاي	kiisush-shaay
teacher	معلم	mu'allim
team (football, etc.)	فريق (كرة قدم الخ)	fariiq (kurat qadam)
teeth	أسنان	asnaan
telephone	هاتف	haatif
to telephone	اتصل	ittasala
can I telephone from here?	هل بالإمكان أن اتصل من هنا؟	hal bil-imkaani an attasila min hinaa?
telephone box	الهاتف العام	al-haatif al-'aam
telephone call	مكالمة هاتفية	makaalamah haatifiyyah
international call	مكالمة دولية	makaalamah duwaliyyah
telephone directory	دليل التلفونات	daliilut-tilifoonaat
television	تلفزيون	tilfizyoon
temperature (fever)	درجة الحرارة (حمى)	darajatul-haraarah (hummaa)

English	Arabic		English	Arabic	
I have a temperature	عندي ارتفاع في درجة الحرارة	'indi irtifaa' fii darajat al-haraarah	thanks	شكراً	shukran
what is the temperature?	ما درجة الحرارة؟	maa darajatul-haraarah?	that	ذلك	thaalika
temporary	مؤقت	mu-aqqat	theatre	مسرح	masrah
tennis	تنس	tenis	there; there is.../there are...	هناك/هناك...	hunaak: hunaaka.../ hunaaka...
I'd like to play tennis	أنا أود أن ألعب التنس	anaa awaddu an al'abat-tenis	is there...?	هل هناك؟	hal hunaaka...?
do you play tennis?	هل تلعب التنس؟	hal tal'abut-tenis?	these	هؤلاء	haa-ulaa
tennis ball	كرة تنس	kuratut-tenis	they	هم	hum
tennis court	ملعب التنس	mal'abut-tenis	thief	لص	lis
tennis racket	مضرب تنس	midrabut-tenis	thin	رقيق	raqiq
tent	خيمة	khaymah	to think	أعتقد	a'taqidu
terrace	شرفة	shurfah	I think so	أعتقد ذلك	a'taqidu thaalika
tetanus	داء الكزاز	daa-ul-kazzaaz	I don't think so	أنا لا أعتقد ذلك	anaa laa a'taqidu thaalika
thank you	شكراً لكم	shaukran lakum	thirsty:	عطشان:أنا عطشان	'atshaan: anaa
			I'm thirsty		'atshaan
			this	هذا	haathaa

English – Arabic

English	Arabic	Transliteration
those	أولئك	ulaa-ika
thread	خيط	khayt
Thursday	الخميس	al-khamiis
ticket	تذكرة	tathkarah
single ticket	تذكرة ذهاب فقط	tathkarat thahaab faqat
return ticket	تذكرة ذهاب وإياب	tathkarat thahaab wa iyaab
ticket office	مكتب التذاكر	maktabut-tathaakir
tie	ربطة العنق	rabdat al-'unuq
tight: it's too tight	ضيق: هو ضيق جداً	dayyiq: huwa dayyiq jiddan
tights	جوارب	jawaarib
time	وقت	waqt
timetable	جدول المواعيد	jadwal al-mawaa'iid
tin opener	مفتاح العلب	miftaah al-'ilab

English	Arabic	Transliteration
tip (to waiter, etc.)	بقشيش (للنادل، إلخ)	baqshiish (lian-naadil)
tired	متعب	mut'ab
tissues	أنسجة	ansigah
to see GRAMMAR	إلى	ilaa
to the station	إلى المحطة	ilal-mahaddah
toast	خبز محمص	khubz muhamas
tobacconist's	بائع السجائر	baa-i' as-sajaa-ir
today	اليوم	al-yawm
together	سوية	sawiyyatan
toilet	مرحاض	mirhaad
toilet paper	ورق المرحاض	waraqul-mirhaad
there is no toilet paper	ليس هناك ورق مرحاض	laysa hunaaka waraq mirhaad
token	نقود	nuquud
toll (on motorway, etc.)	ضريبة (على الطريق السريع، إلخ)	thariibah ('alat-tariiq as-saarii')

English	Arabic		English	Arabic	
tomato	طماطم	tamaatim	tough (meat)	غير ناضج (اللحم)	qayr nadij (lahm)
tomato juice	عصير الطماطم	'asiirut-tamaatim	tour	جولة	jawlah
tomato salad	سلطة طماطم	saltat tamaatim	tourist	سائح	saa-ih
tomorrow	غدا	qadan	tourist office	مكتب السياحة	maktabus-siyaahah
tomorrow morning	صباح الغد	sabaahal-qad	towel	منشفة	minshafah
tomorrow evening	مساء الغد	masaa-al-qad	tower	برج	burj
tonight	الليلة	allaylah	town	بلدة	baldah
tooth	سن	sin	town hall	دار البلدية	daarul-baladiyyah
toothache	وجع الأسنان	waja'al-asnaan	toy	لعبة	lu'bah
toothbrush	فرشاة الأسنان	furshaatul-asnaan	traditional	تقليدي	taqliidii
toothpaste	معجون الأسنان	ma'juunul-asnaan	traffic	مرور	muruur
torch (electric)	مصباح (كهربائي)	misbaah (kahrubaa-ii)	traffic lights	إشارات المرور	ishaaratul-muruur
total	مجموع	majmuu'	train	قطار	qitaar
			trainers (shoes)	أحذية جري (حذاء)	ah-thiyat jari
			to translate	ترجم	tarjama
			to travel	سافر	saafara

English - Arabic

English	Arabic	Transliteration
travel agent	وكيل السفريات	wakilus-safariyyaat
traveller's cheques	صكوك المسافرين	sukuukul-musaafiriin
tree	شجرة	shajarah
trip: a day trip	رحلة: رحلة نهارية	rihlah: rihla nahaariyyah
trousers	بنطلون	bantaloon
trout	تراوت	trawt
truck	شاحنة	shaahinah
true: that's true	حقيقة: هذه حقيقة	haqiiqah: haathihiil-haqiiqah
that's not true	هذه ليست حقيقة	haathihii laysat haqiiqah
trunks (swimming)	بنطلون سباحة (سباحة)	bantaloon sibaahah (sibaahah)
try on: can I try it on?	جرب: هل بالإمكان ان اجربه على؟	jarraba: hal bil-imkaani an ujarribahu 'alay?
t-shirt	فانلة	faanillah
Tuesday	الثلاثاء	ath-thulaa
tuna	سمك التونة	samakut-tuunah
tunnel	نفق	nafaq
turkey	الديك الرومي	addiikur-ruumii
Turkish bath	الحمام التركي	al-hammaam at-turki
to turn off (radio, light)	أطفأ (راديو، ضو)	atfa-a (raadyoo, daw)
to turn on	فتح	fataha
tweezers	ملقط	milqad
twins	توأم	taw-am
U		
ugly	قبيح	qabiih
umbrella	شمسية	shamsiyyah

English	Arabic	
uncomfortable	مزعج	muz'ij
to understand	فهم	fahima
I don't understand	أنا لا أفهم	anaa laa afham
do you understand?	هل تفهم؟	hal tafham?
underwear	ملابس داخلية	malaabis daakhiliyyah
unemployed	عاطل	'aatil
university	جامعة	jaami'ah
unleaded petrol	البنزين الخالي من الرصاص	al-binzin al-khaali minar-rasaas
unlucky	سيئ الحظ	say-yi'-ul hath
upstairs	الطابق العلوي	at-taabiq al-'ulwii
urgent: it's urgent	هذا مستعجل	mustaʿjil: haathaa mustaʿjil

English	Arabic	
to use	استعمال	ista'mala
useful	مفيد	mufid
usually	عادة	haadatan
V		
vacancy (room)	شاغر (غرفة)	shaaqir (qurfah)
valid	صحيح	sahiih
valuables	الأشياء الثمينة	al-ashyaa ath-thamiinah
van	شاحنة	shaa-hinah
VAT	ضريبة	thariibah
veal	لحم العجل	lahmul-'ijl
vegetable	خضار	khuthaar
vegetarian	نباتي	nabaatii
very	جدا	jiddan
very good	جيد جدا	jayid jiddan
view	منظر	manthar
village	قرية	qaryah
vineyard	مزرعة العنب	mazra'atul-'inab

English – Arabic

English – Arabic

visa	ta-shiirah	تأشيرة
to visit	zaara	زار
visitor	zaa-ir	زائر
W		
to wait (for)	intathara	انتظر (على)
please wait	ar-rajaa al-intithaar	الرجاء الانتظار
waiter/waitress	naadil/naadilah	نادل/نادلة
waiting room	qurfatul-intithaar	غرفة الانتظار
to wake up	istayqatha	استيقظ
Wales	wilz	ويلز
to walk	mashaa	مشى
walk (activity); (route)	mashaa (nashaat); (tariiq)	مشي (نشاط)؛ (طريق)
walking stick	'ukkaazah	عكّازة
wallet	mahfathah	محفظة
to want	araada	أراد

war	harb	حرب
wardrobe	khizaanah	خزانة
warm	daafi	دافئ
to wash	qasala	غسل
washbasin	hawth al-qasil	حوض الغسيل
washing machine	qassaalah	غسّالة
washing powder	mashuuqul-qasiil	مسحوق الغسيل
wasp	zanbuur	زنبور
watch (wrist)	sahaat (risq)	ساعة (رسغ)
water	maa	ماء
mineral water	maa ma'dani	ماء معدني
fresh water	maa athb	ماء عذب
waterfall	shallaal	شلال
waterproof	mi'taf	معطف
water-skiing	attazahluq 'alaal-maa	التزحلق على الماء

wave	موجه	mawjah	*last week*	الأسبوع الماضي	al-isbuu' al-maathii
way: is this the right way?	الطريق: هل هذا هو الطريق الصحيح؟	attariiq: hal haathaa huwat-tariiq?	*next week*	الأسبوع القادم	al-isbuu' al-qaadim
way out	خرج	makhhraj	weekend	عطلة نهاية الأسبوع	'utlat nihaayat al-usbuu'
we	نحن	nahnu			
weak (tea, coffee, drink, etc.)	خفيف (شاي، قهوة، شراب)	khafiif (shaay, qahwah, sharaab)	weekly	اسبوعي	isbuu'ii
			weight	وزن	wazn
to wear	لبس	labisa	welcome!	مرحبا!	marhabaa!
weather forecast	توقعات حالة الطقس	tawaqqu'aat haalatut-taqs	well	حسنا	hasanan
			well done (meat)	مطهي جيدا (لحم)	hathii jayyidan (lahm)
wedding	زفاف	zafaaf	west	غرب	qarb
wedding ring	خاتم الزواج	khaatamuz-zawaaj	wet	مبلول	mabluul
			wetsuit	ملابس الغوص	malaabis al-qaws
Wednesday	الأربعاء	al-arbi'aa	what	ما	maa
week	أسبوع	isbuu'	*what is it?*	ما هو؟	maa haathaa?

English – Arabic

English – Arabic

wheelchair	كرسي المعوقين	kursiyyul-mu'awwaqiin
when?	متى؟	mataa?
where?	أين؟	atna?
which?	أي؟	ayyu?
which one?	أي واحد؟	ayyu waahid?
white	أبيض	abyad
who	من	man
whole	كل	kulli
whose:	لمن: لمن	liman: liman
whose is it?	لمن هذا؟	haathaa?
why	لماذا	limaathaa
wife	زوجة	zawjah
window	نافذة (بيت)؛ (دكّان)	naafithah (bayt); (dukkaan)
(house); (shop)		
windsurfing	ركوب الرياح	rukuubur-riyaah
windy:	عاصف؛ الجو	'aasif: al-jawwu
it's windy	عاصف	'aasif

wine	نبيذ	nabiid
red wine	النبيذ الأحمر	annabiid al-ahmar
white wine	النبيذ الأبيض	annabiid al-abyad
wine list	قائمة النبيذ	qaa-imat annabiid
the wine list, please	قائمة النبيذ رجاءً	qaa-imat annabiid, rajaa-an
winter	شتاء	shitaa
with	مع	ma'a
without	بدون	bidoon
woman	امرأة	imra-ah
wood (substance)	خشب (مادة)	khashab (maaddah)
word	كلمة	kalimah
to work	عمل	'amila

English		Arabic
it doesn't work	huwa laa ya'mal	هو لا يعمل
to write	kataba	كتب
writing paper	waraqul-litaabah	ورق الكتابة
wrong	khaati	خاطئ
X		
x-ray	al-ashi'ah assiiniyyah	الأشعة السينية
Y		
yacht	mirkab	مركب
year	sanah	سنة
this year	haathihis-sanah	هذه السنة
yellow	asfar	أصفر
yes	na'am	نعم
yesterday	ams	أمس
you	anta	أنت
youth hostel	funduq ash-shabaab	فندق الشباب
Z		
zero	sifr	صفر
zip	arramz al-bariidii	الرمز البريدي
zoo	hadiiqatul-hayawaanaat	حديقة الحيوانات

English – Arabic

Further titles in Collins' phrasebook range
Collins Gem Phrasebook

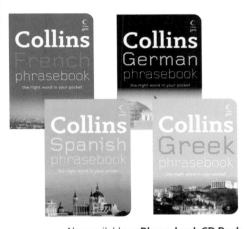

Also available as **Phrasebook CD Pack**
Other titles in the series

Arabic	Greek	Polish
Cantonese	Italian	Portuguese
Croatian	Japanese	Russian
Czech	Korean	Spanish
Dutch	Latin American	Thai
French	Spanish	Turkish
German	Mandarin	Vietnamese

Collins Phrasebook & Dictionary

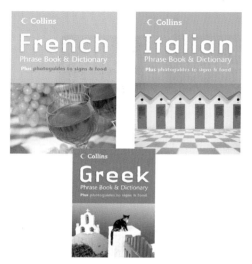

Also available as **Phrasebook CD Pack**
Other titles in the series
German Japanese Portuguese Spanish

Collins Easy: Photo Phrasebook

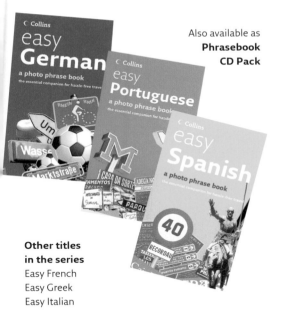

Also available as
**Phrasebook
CD Pack**

**Other titles
in the series**
Easy French
Easy Greek
Easy Italian

To order any of these titles, please telephone
0870 787 1732. For further information about all
Collins books, visit our website: www.collins.co.uk